Beyond the School Gate

When Being a Mum is Not Enough

MICHELLE KUKLINSKI

First published by Busybird Publishing 2016
Copyright © 2016 Michelle Kuklinski
ISBN
Print: 978-1-925585-03-2
Ebook: 978-1-925585-04-9

Michelle Kuklinski has asserted her right under the Copyright, Designs and Patents Act 1988 to be identified as the author of this work. The information in this book is based on the author's experiences and opinions. The publisher specifically disclaims responsibility for any adverse consequences, which may result from use of the information contained herein. Permission to use information has been sought by the author. Any breaches will be rectified in further editions of the book.

All rights reserved. No part of this publication may be reproduced, stored in or introduced into a retrieval system, or transmitted in any form, or by any means (electronic, mechanical, photocopying, recording or otherwise) without the prior written permission of the author. Any person who does any unauthorised act in relation to this publication may be liable to criminal prosecution and civil claims for damages. Enquiries should be made through the publisher.

Cover image: Kev Howlett, Busybird Publishing
Cover design: Busybird Publishing
Layout and typesetting: Busybird Publishing
Editor: Busybird Publishing

Busybird Publishing
PO Box 855
Eltham Victoria
Australia 3095
www.busybird.com.au

Testimonial

I was excited when I heard Michelle was writing a book because I know she has so much wisdom and experience to share. Michelle and I have worked together in both a personal and professional capacity. As a coach, Michelle always provides a safe space to explore ideas and delve more deeply than first thought possible, always believing in her client's ability to change and grow.

Michelle's commitment to her own personal development and growth means she always has new strategies and tools to share with her clients. Michelle's book will allow so many people to access ideas and principles that will enable them to move forward with more options and more confidence, creating the change they desire.
    – Annie Garner

To Dylan and Layla,

You are my reason.

To Diete,

In recognition of your strength, your love and your creativity.

To Ian,

For always giving me my freedom.

To Paul TM,

For your unwavering friendship and support – words will never suffice.

And to my amazing family and friends who have contributed to who I am today, I am so very grateful to have you in my life.

Contents

Introduction	i
1. Shining that Spotlight on You	1
2. Get Your Mojo Working	9
3. Who's Running Your Show?	17
4. Getting to the Heart of YOU	25
5. Pick Yourself Up and Dust Yourself Down	37
6. Hiring the Right Home Help	45
7. Yoga for the Mind	55
8. Picking Your Team	63
9. Adult Conversations	71
10. On a Mission to Succeed	79
11. Thinking Outside the Box	87
12. Calling in the Experts	97
Afterword	105
Testimonials (continued)	107
About the Author	111
Exclusive Offer	113

Introduction

Are you a mother who gave up your corporate gig to be there for your family? Perhaps you've made the decision that you no longer want what your previous career entailed but you know that something is missing.

You love your children – that is not in doubt – but surely there has to be more than this endless round of school runs, after-school clubs and packing lunches. You feel disconnected from who you used to be and lost in the label of motherhood. Who am I now and what is my purpose beyond my children? Instead of getting answers, you find yourself spiralling in doubt, frustration and confusion.

I've been there. I had no desire to go back to full-time work. It just wasn't a good fit for my children. I struggled with what I saw as the monotonous and relentless side of being a mum. I longed for different stimulation and life outside of being a mum. I also wanted to create my own income, not just to contribute to the household, but as a way of feeling independent from my home role.

Being the person I am and having a supportive network of family and friends, I came through the frustration. I created different opportunities, experimented and earned an income. But most importantly, I gave myself the opportunity to accept who I am and what I needed in my life without feeling guilty.

Of course, I am still a mum, but that alone does not define me. It is just a part of me. It was a struggle and it took time to become a more authentic version of me. Through my coaching journey, I have seen how I could have better utilised my tenacity and come to this place much sooner than I did.

With my knowledge and coaching expertise, I'm determined to make a difference by helping women to enable themselves to create a more positive life. I have accomplished many different goals and so can you. I just want you to get there quicker than I did.

Don't get me wrong, there are plenty of women out there who are absolutely content with being completely absorbed in motherhood. I respect that and I'm often in awe of those women. But I am not that woman and I know that there are many of you out there who are not either so this book is for you.

I understand the guilt, the self-doubt and the constant critical voice in your head saying that you're not enough. This book is designed to identify and bring you out of that self-destructive pattern, how to change it and, more importantly, to give you the steps to identify and create the life you want and the independence from that label of motherhood which you deserve.

Whether it's finding an interest or creating a microbusiness to generate an income, this book, with its easy and actionable steps, will help you achieve this and more. I've written this book to be a course that will give you enough steps and guidance to get you started on your personal journey.

I understand that for some this may seem a little challenging and, as such, each chapter can stand alone as a resource where you can dip in and out and still achieve great results. Picking yourself up from underneath that washing pile might seem immense but it doesn't need to be. So, pick a chapter, take a deep breath and jump in.

You can often change your circumstances by changing your attitude.

– Eleanor Roosevelt

1. Shining that Spotlight on You
– Creating a Positive Mindset

If you're reading this book, then chances are that you know what it is that you don't want. But have you actually stopped to think about what it is that you do want? To kick things off, I'm going to talk about where your focus is and changing it to create a positive mindset.

The coaching adage is: what you focus on is what you get. And it's true. As a simple example, think about when you last purchased a car. Afterwards, all you see on the road is that particular model whereas you probably had less awareness of it before.

Now, think about your normal day. You get caught up in – that is, focusing on – the school runs, packed lunches, after-school activities and what you're cooking for dinner. Chances are that your mindset is, *God, this is so boring; I'm going to scream if my child asks me what's for dinner tonight.* You are sick of having the contents of your larder in your head, so you're constantly focusing on the negative and what you would rather not be doing instead of what it is you really want to be doing.

When you change your focus and get a clear idea of how you want your day to be, it starts to stimulate new and creative ways of thinking. This opens your mind to new possibilities. It gives clarity and lifts the fog. You think, *Hey, that's possible, I can do that so let's look into this more.*

It also brings acceptance of who you are today is not who you were before having your kids. In other words, what's important has probably changed. When my son was born, I was determined that having a child wasn't going to change my life dramatically, that I could still go out clubbing and do all my pre-child 'things'. I tried really hard!

The first couple of times I thought that it was fine but then I realised that it wasn't worth it. I was just grumpy the next day and I couldn't handle things. Gradually, my interests changed and past interests lost their appeal. I had moved on but I did battle for a while, focusing on what I thought I should want based on an old version of me rather than focusing on what it was I wanted in the here-and-now.

It can be a shock realising that a few years have gone by (and you are not sure how) and that who you were one or two or even ten years ago is just not who you are today. Also, changing your focus and having a good mindset about where you want to head energises you into creating change.

Think about it. You focus on how you want your day to be; for example, to spend two hours a day doing a new hobby. As you visualise and plan, your whole physiology lifts and you think, *Yeah that's what I'm going to do. So ok, how am I going to do that? I'm going to look at a course list and research it.*

As you implement action towards your goals, you feel energised rather than drained because you are positively focusing on what you want as opposed to what you don't want.

If you don't have the chance to develop a positive mindset, then you're not going to move beyond your current emotional and physical state. This will negatively impact on those around you as well as yourself. You're not going to enjoy or even notice the good times as you become resentful and lose the ability to see anything outside of where you are choosing to look. Seeing all that is negative becomes a downhill spiral and a habit that can be hard to break.

What exactly do I mean by 'focus'? In coaching terms, what you choose to focus on is what you will see, achieve and experience to the exclusion of anything else. The mind does not distinguish between negatives and positives so it will just search out for the evidence to support what you are focusing on.

If you focus on your lack of time, your mind will look for and give you the evidence to support it so all you see is your rushing about, feeling tired and people making too many demands. It's like a torch. When you shine that torch onto an object, you will not see anything peripheral to that beam of light. That's your focus. You have to expand that beam or move it to look at something else.

What to Do: Step 1

So, you are ready to change your focus and develop a great mindset.

First off, invest time exploring your ideal, sustainable day. Be specific about the day from the moment you get up to when you go to bed.

Invoke all of your senses: your sights, your sounds, what you're feeling and who you're seeing. I'm not talking about a day on a tropical island drinking cocktails. I'm talking about a day you can do consistently.

At what time do you want to get up? Who do you want to see in the morning? What foods do you want to eat? Who do you want to talk to? What sort of conversations do you want to have? What do your surroundings look like? Where are you living?

Be really specific and you will gain some clarity about how you want your day to be. Be imaginative. Once you focus on what it is you want, you will look for ways to make it happen. And don't forget to write it all down!

What to Do: Step 2

To help change your focus and create more positivity – yes, I'm going to say it – I recommend you keep a journal. I have thought long and hard about this one as there is a bit of a 'gratitude journal' bandwagon going on at the moment. For reasons I am more than happy to discuss outside of this book, I am dropping the word 'gratitude' but I do want you to start a journal nonetheless and give it a name that resonates with you.

My rules are simple:

1. Only happy things go in.

2. Mix it up. Use words, pictures, photos, texture and colour to make it uniquely yours.

3. Do it consistently. It may be everyday or once a week but be consistent.

4. Enjoy.

The entries need not be huge things like winning the lottery but can be small things that surround you and put a smile on your face. It might have been a word that your child said to you or it might be a drawing which they gave you.

I've treasured letters from my daughter that go into my journal. I have a photo of hanging lights at a night market that lifted my spirits. It's like a life journal but only positive things are in it. It makes you think about what you already have in your life and what you enjoy. Think of it as a present to yourself and maybe also to your family if you are happy to share it.

What to Do: Step 3

Finally, don't just take my word for it. Have a go for yourself! Go in big and think of a time when you had a huge change in your life, or when you tried to do something and it didn't work the first time but then you changed your approach and it did work.

The first time my husband and I tried to get our Australian residency, we attempted the paperwork ourselves but failed at the first hurdle. We came to the conclusion that it was too complicated and that it wasn't going to happen.

A year or so later I went to a travel expo and there were agents who specialised in getting visas to other countries. After a conversation with them and watching a film about Australia, my focus completely changed. These guys did visa applications for a living and it was a 'no visa, no fee' arrangement so, as far as I was concerned, we were getting the visa. We just needed to follow their instructions.

My focus was purely on what was the next step needed and my mindset was that we were getting the visa. Sure enough, we got our residency. That was about me changing my focus, looking for a way to achieve the outcome and being determined that we were coming to Australia no matter what.

Take something in your life now that you want to change. Be specific on your outcome and start looking for the evidence to support your outcome and act as if it will happen. In my case, I wanted to migrate to Australia. I researched and used migration experts and I said 'when' the visa comes through, not 'if'. I acted as if it was a done deal.

See? What you focus on is what you get.

Nice Try but I've Heard It Before

My clients often say to me that they feel stuck and can't imagine their life being any different.

Everyone has the capacity to imagine after a little prompting. I've yet to come across someone who has no imagination or the capacity to visualise. Change the language if necessary. Call it 'daydreaming' or 'storytelling' if it helps. Turn it into a game. Make up a positive fairy story to regale to your children then turn the heroine of the story into you.

Another objection I've had is that people are afraid of change and like who they are currently. Yet, if you stop to think about it, we are never the same person doing the same thing. We evolve and change to our circumstances. Quite frankly, would you want to be the person you were years ago with less knowledge and experience?

We are not talking about a complete personality or life swap (unless that's what you want) but a means of addressing how you can see things differently and achieve your ideal day and life.

Another thing that I've had thrown at me is, 'If I tried changing my life, who is going to run the house and kids?'

Well, we're not talking about getting rid of the house or the kids. Of course, they're an important part of your life. But as you create change, you will start to see possibilities and solutions.

For example, you want to go and do an evening class. You may chat about it to another mum and she also wants a free evening. Before you know it, you've agreed to exchange babysitting which gives both of you some free time.

> **Your Key Actions and Learnings**
> 1. Design your ideal day.
>
> 2. Start a journal and only use positive focus.
>
> 3. Start changing your focus and see the results that you achieve.

My mission in life is not to survive, but to thrive; and to do so with some passion, some compassion, some humour and some style.

Maya Angelou

2. Get Your Mojo Working
– Finding Your Passion

Without passion, you're not living the full version of you. You are merely existing. That may sound harsh but I'm guessing that your mojo has disappeared, otherwise you wouldn't be wondering what is happening to your life or wanting to know how you'll find yourself again.

I've been there and I know what it can feel like. For me, it felt like there was something lurking at the top of a cupboard that I had to really stretch up to find and, just when my fingers seemed to touch it, it would fall down the back. Then I would sink back down onto the floor wondering what the hell had just happened.

For most people, finding their passion is not an instant one-step fix. Just like cooking, quick fixes are rarely a great experience. Think of the instant potato mix that you just add water to. It's a poor imitation of real mashed potatoes. Spending the time to prep, using good ingredients and a little experimentation with the recipe ... that's when the magic happens.

When you find your passion, you've got your reason to get up in the morning with a spring in your step. When your passion gives you purpose, it helps you cope with the stuff that doesn't drive you so much. It gives you the courage and the energy to push past obstacles and tackle setbacks.

If you're not having a good day at home, you cope with that because you know for half of that day or evening you're following your passion. That outlook brightens up your whole day. Life becomes more satisfying as you have a genuine interest that you're choosing to follow and to immerse yourself in.

Having passion opens you up to opportunities that you didn't see before. As you look down avenues to pursue your passion, new doors open, you meet different people and you discover different things.

It's a bit like a real-life internet search as you meet one person which then leads to a conversation followed by an introduction to another person who knows about something else. Soon, it's snowballing and there's a multitude of opportunities and experiences coming your way.

As you get more into your passion, you'll notice how it lifts your mood, which has a knock-on effect on your physiology. You start to dress differently, you move differently and you seem more radiant, confident and relaxed. People then comment on that 'difference' which further reinforces your positive psychological state.

As you become more positive and confident, you attract those type of people because like attracts like. Think about the times in your life when you've been a bit down and the sort of conversations you've had. You were probably talking to people who were moaning, whinging and being negative because you were attracting that.

Think of a time when you were feeling positive and the sorts of people you were talking to. Can you see the difference?

As you attract more positivity, the conversations you have will change and you gain more knowledge. Your mind expands, you become more stimulated and you become an expert in your chosen area. You then become even more interesting than you already are as you have gained a new facet to your personality.

A lot of people seem to think that passion is something that will materialise out of thin air. For most, it doesn't. Clients expect to click their fingers and have passion ignited as if by magic. You'll be waiting a long time if that is your approach. You need to be open to experience. Have an open mind and interact. Be curious and take action.

To not have a passion, a real and true interest, is to deny yourself fulfilment and a successful life. You become a 'second best' version of yourself. What sort of example are you setting for your children? I imagine that as a parent, you want the best for them and you encourage them to be the best. And who better to show them than you giving them a great model to follow? You owe it not just to your children but also to yourself.

What do I mean by 'passion'? For me, it's the fuel that drives you and the vision for your life. It's based on your most important values, strengths, skills and talents. In other words, your uniqueness. It's also a state of being. You 'feel' your passion like a physical entity; your eyes light up when you speak about it, your heart rate accelerates, you get goose bumps, you glow, you feel engaged and stimulated and you 'just know' it's meant to be.

I understand that it can be a confusing path to finding your passion, so here are three steps to help you.

What to Do: Step 1

Stop falling into things. Whilst passion may not come to you instantly, take ownership and start defining your journey to finding it. Don't do things for the sake of it. Do it because you want to do it and because there is a purpose behind it, whether it's a step towards your goal or embracing a project as a whole.

Instead of asking yourself, *What am I passionate about?* try asking, *What can I do with my time that is important?* Use your past to get clues and insights. What did you love doing as a child? What was it you loved about your jobs? What filled your spare time before children? Where did you go? Who did you interact with? What sort of films did you like? Who did you admire and why?

What to Do: Step 2

Start a journal and write down words and single sentences. Use these to make connections. Draw pictures if that works for you. There's no right or wrong or even any sense to it. Freewheel it and connections will appear in the most random way, which is what you want.

Be creative in your thinking. When I relayed to someone that I used to truant from school a lot and travel the underground to explore different places, their immediate response was that I was clearly resourceful. I had never looked at it that way and it sure sounded a lot better than the story I had been telling myself! What can your connections and memories mean? Draw out the positive.

As a teenager, I loved hanging around London's Covent Garden and spent hours in The Bead Shop trawling through beads, picking up different colours, then going home and making stuff out of my purchases.

Somewhere along the path of life, I stopped and it was a couple of decades before I went back to that and developed my jewellery-making skills. When I reflected on those teenage years, I realised how many of those things that I now enjoy and embrace in differing contexts can be traced back to then.

What to Do: Step 3

You have got to **TAKE ACTION**. This is important. Yes, I'm yelling this one as I really want you to take this onboard. Unless you immerse yourself in the 'doing', you're not going to experience the 'having'. You cannot think your way into a passion. You have 'do' your way into a passion.

It doesn't have to be a huge action to start with. It can be as simple as going to a library and getting a 'how to' book or looking at what classes are available in your area. Over time, those steps get bigger, you discover what works and what doesn't, what you want to continue to discover and what can be put in the 'this isn't working for me' pile.

Look at creative sites such as Pinterest which have guides for how to create things and Etsy to see how and what creative stuff people are selling. Read blogs and join interest groups. There are all sorts of ways to prompt you into action. Look out for what gets you excited and what makes you think, *Wow, I'd love to do that.* These are all clues.

I turned my rediscovery of jewellery into a small business and that only happened as a result of taking action. I did classes to learn different skills, I researched suppliers, I bought books and looked at websites to get inspiration and, most importantly, I put myself out there. And I still get the hugest buzz when someone wants to buy my creations!

Finally, ask others! Sometimes, those looking from the outside can see what you cannot. Chat to family, friends or even ex-colleagues. How do they perceive you? What do they see as your traits and qualities? What do you do well? What do they love about you? What do you take from that feedback?

Sometimes, you can't see the wood for the trees and that can be true of yourself. You will probably hear things that will take you by surprise or may affirm that you are on the right path.

Whilst I tend to have a good sense of what I do and don't like, having other people's comments and feedback has given me a confidence boost to do things that I may otherwise have just left as a dream and later regret. Listen to what people say to you and link that into what you love about life and what you think you would like to do.

Nice Try but I've Heard It Before

Sometimes, people can feel overwhelmed as they have so many ideas and don't know how to refine it down to one idea.

You don't have to limit yourself to one idea. You can be absolutely passionate about several things. You are not a one-dimensional object but a wonderful mix of many facets, just like a shining diamond!

I am passionate about my business and what that entails but that is not the sum of me. I have many personal interests, some of which overlap into my business and an awful lot which do not.

Have fun exploring your ideas and see what recurring themes come up in your daily life and whether there are overlaps into other areas. Quiet often, people convince themselves that there is nothing they feel passionate about and assume that a mundane life is their lot.

I believe that everyone can have passion and be passionate. Just remember that it can be a slow, simmering pot that needs a bit of stirring and seasoning rather than the immediacy of a flaming pudding!

Sometimes, there is guilt associated with admitting that your current life is unfulfilling and that guilt can hold you back. But it is fine to want something else. Also, what does passion mean to you? Are you giving it your meaning or an external meaning that has no relevance to you?

The old chestnut of not having enough time comes up a lot and my response is always the same: how important is this to you? There are always five or ten minutes you can find. Be creative.

Cook a dinner that you can do off pat – spaghetti Bolognese is always a good one – and let your mind wander as you cook. Put the kids in front of the television for half an hour to give you some space to write. This won't kill them if only done occasionally. Walk round the block and utilise the voice memo on your phone to record ideas. Take yourself away from your distractions by going to bed ten minutes earlier; have a pad by your bed and use those ten minutes to jot down ideas.

Where there is a will, there is a way.

> ## **Your Key Actions and Learnings**
> 1. Take ownership and start defining your journey.
>
> 2. Start a 'clue' journal.
>
> 3. Take action, whether small or large, but just **take action.**

Face your deficiencies and acknowledge them; but do not let them master you. Let them teach you patience, sweetness, insight.

Helen Keller

3. Who's Running Your Show?
– *Examining Your Beliefs*

As we get caught up in the melee of family life, there comes a moment when we wonder who we are now, mourning for who we were and where we are heading. Whilst parts of our identity are fairly non-negotiable, such as gender, most of our identity is made up of beliefs which are unique and based on our life experiences along with cultural or societal expectations.

Recognising what beliefs will support you positively is the key in creating change. Why is that? By identifying the beliefs you have enables you to change the ones that are not serving your purpose and to be clear on the positive ones that are. Some are going to hold you back, whereas others will propel you forward.

Beliefs influence how you perceive yourself and the world around you, so by changing some of your beliefs or creating new ones, you influence your thinking and your behaviour and therefore your results and responses.

For example, if you hold the belief that stay-at-home mums have to do all the housework because they are not going to work, then chances are that belief is going to make you feel like a bit of a drudge unless your adore housework.

However, if you change that belief to 'I do a full-time job with the kids', then the knock-on effect is that you believe housework is a joint responsibility since both parents work but just in different arenas. Then you might be prepared to negotiate and discuss how that housework is more fairly distributed which ends up giving you free time.

Beliefs affect what we choose to focus on, which can limit you. Given that we focus on finding evidence to support our beliefs, then if you change the belief, you change the focus. A general belief is that women are nurturers, so all you see are mothers caring for children to the exclusion of anything else. But if one believes that anyone can have a nurturing nature, then you will observe both fathers and mothers who are fantastic with children. This has opened up your focus and you see the world differently.

Some beliefs serve to keep you 'safe'; that is, to be stuck or not living authentically. You might conform to your peer groups' expectations because you fear being ridiculed. You would rather subjugate your values and beliefs than follow what you believe to be true.

Finding the courage to be 'you' will ultimately attract you to like-minded people who are more in line with your values and will genuinely accept you for who you are.

Great things are achieved when you step away from being safe. Changing your beliefs can have a huge impact on your emotional and physical wellbeing. Physical symptoms such as headaches, muscle tension, anxiety can be due to unfair pressure we put on ourselves through negative beliefs. Just as having a massage releases tension, changing beliefs can have the power to bring relief and healing.

Many people have the notion that beliefs are facts, but they're not, which means they're open to change.

If you choose to live with unsupportive beliefs, then you continue down the same path of being stuck at where you're at. You're giving into staying safe and remaining rigid in your lifestyle. You won't be open to new ways of thinking and experiencing the world. You're choosing to place mental limitations on yourself, which in turn limits your life choices and impacts your physical health.

Let's be clear: a belief is something that we believe to be true. Beliefs are built on our experiences and interactions with the external world, which we then filter. We choose what we agree with, change them, delete them and then internalise these beliefs as part of our psyche.

What to Do: Step 1

What can we do in looking at our beliefs? One thing is to examine the key areas in your life, such as relationships, health and finances. Write down what your beliefs are, using statements such as 'I believe that …' or 'I think that …' or 'I'm certain that …' or 'I doubt that …'

Remember there's no right or wrong. This is for your eyes only. When you've written down those statements, have a look at them. What could be limiting you and holding you back? What are the great beliefs that will serve you?

When I was completing my degree, I endlessly procrastinated when an essay was due. I had a list of tasks that I thought I had to do, such as cleaning the oven and my oven has never looked as clean before or since! I told myself that I couldn't do the essay before I had completed this list and that these tasks were more important than my essay. When I looked at it honestly, I had the belief that writing content was hard and that I didn't know what to write.

That belief wasn't serving me. It wasn't until I thought about the actual task in hand and how I felt at the end of it that I recognised how energised I felt when I was thinking and writing creatively. I loved the feeling that I got once I had completed an essay. I just got a huge buzz out of it.

So I changed my belief to one where written tasks energise me and that knowledge will come to me in the writing process. That gave me the impetus to start rather than to procrastinate.

What to Do: Step 2

Your behaviour and emotions are key clues to your beliefs. Examine what triggers a strong response and then ask why. You have a set of rules which support your beliefs and which govern your behaviour and responses to other people's behaviour.

For example, it might be important to you that you are punctual because your belief is that people who are late do not respect others. Therefore, you and others must always be on time. If that rule is rigid – in other words, if you have no flexibility – then chances are that it will really wind you up if someone is late to meet you even if they have a legitimate excuse.

Key identifiers that you are engaging rigid rules are using sentences which include words such as 'ought to', 'have to' and 'must do'.

I used to constantly beat myself up about my perceived inadequacies of being a mother based on my beliefs on what being a good mother encompassed. I thought that I should be more patient, more caring, make meals into works of art like animal sandwiches on three different types of bread, send my children to more after-school activities – you name it, I could find fault and would constantly look at what I wasn't doing rather than what I was doing. As a consequence of my perceptions, I could be quite judgemental on other mothers. It was my strategy to make myself feel better.

Eventually, I knew I had to change my beliefs around what being a mother meant to me. I had to stop self-sabotaging and stop being excessively critical. Now I have a more laid back approach, believing that we all do the best we can with what we have. And that is good enough. We do not need to be perfect.

What to Do: Step 3

Don't get me wrong, changing your beliefs can feel unfamiliar. You've probably spent a considerable number of years and invested a lot of time in your specific beliefs so it's normal to experience a degree of awkwardness.

Having the mantra that nothing has meaning but the meaning you give it may help. This was a game changer for me. It was very powerful and liberating and it gave me freedom.

What exactly do I mean by this? Well, how we look at things varies. Two people can be in the same situation but will give a different version of their experience and their experience is true to them. Two people in a restaurant eating the same meal are not going to have the same opinion of that meal.

Both might have liked it but one preferred one aspect of the meal to the other. One preferred dessert to the main course or one found the waiter provided good service whereas the other might pick on it. Both were in the same situation but both had a different experience of it.

The same is true of your beliefs. It is you and only you who give the meaning to anything you believe in. Think of driving your car and then you hear the driver behind you tooting you. What do you choose to make that mean? Do you decide that the person is being rude and impatient? Are they warning you that something is up with your car? Do you assume they know you? See where I am going with this? You can change the meaning. Nothing is cast in stone and nothing has meaning except the meaning you give it.

You have the power to change your beliefs and it's not about challenging what others hold true but what you hold true. Nothing has to be static. Things can constantly evolve and change according to what's needed. You might change your belief and, a year later, you might need to change it or tweak it and that is absolutely fine.

When I entered motherhood, my belief was that my lifestyle did not have to change. But it did and as long as I held that belief, I experienced frustration and depression. Once I looked at that belief and changed it – that motherhood is about adapting and that adapting does not mean the loss of what I love doing but adjusting how it's achieved – then I felt more content.

Nice Try but I've Heard It Before

What if my partner, family and friends don't agree with my new beliefs?

In my experience and that of my clients, changing your beliefs will often have a positive impact on those around you.

Nonetheless, some friends will drop by the wayside. But chances are they were fair-weather friends anyway and that would have happened at some stage. With family members, it can shake the status quo and may take time to adjust but an honest conversation is probably the best way to deal with this.

Another thing my clients say to me is, 'I don't have negative beliefs.'

Fantastic! Then I trust you're living the life you truly want. However, it never hurts to review your beliefs every now and again.

Still, others say, 'But I don't know what beliefs I should be changing.'

Trust that you do know. Look for signs such as frustration, being too rigid and not accepting and listening to other people's points of view. Are you experiencing stress or unwelcomed physical symptoms? Are some people avoiding you or always changing the conversation you are having? What is it you're telling yourself in those moments? They're all signifiers or little prompts around the beliefs you might need to change.

Your Key Actions and Learnings

1. Examine your beliefs. Pick a key area in your life such as relationships or money and write down as many as you can. Highlight the positive supporting beliefs. Look at how you can change the negative beliefs.

2. What are you not doing? What are you procrastinating about? Look beyond the excuses and see what you are choosing to believe.

3. Be conscious of your reactions on a day-to-day basis. What are your beliefs in those moments?

There was something wrong with her. She did not know what it was but there was something wrong with her. A hunger, a restlessness. An incomplete knowledge of herself. The sense of something farther away, beyond her reach.

Chimamanda Ngozi Adichie, *Half of a Yellow Sun*

4. Getting to the Heart of YOU

– *Your Personality Recipe*

Deep down, we all love hearing about ourselves. I think that is why astrology and Chinese signs are so popular because we can pick out bits of our personality and connect with the intangible that legitimises who we are and our behaviour. It gives us a reason for why we behave the way we do. We've all heard that line, 'Well, I'm a <insert star sign> so of course I do X, Y, Z.'

As fascinating and fun as this is, basing your behaviour and personality on these 'traits' does not give you ownership and presupposes that you cannot change the way you behave or respond to situations.

There is a plethora of psychology theories which seek to explain human behaviour and, whilst most have merit, their academic approach tends not to lend itself to those seeking a simple and clear understanding.

Human behaviour and thought is complex and contradictory. The root cause of this paradox is based on the simple needs which Abraham Maslow suggested with his hierarchy of needs in his paper, *A Theory of Human Motivation*, first published in 1943. Maslow's model of human needs continue to be utilised in mainstream society, contributing to educational teaching and classroom management. In the self-development arena, coach and speaker Tony Robbins developed '6 Core Human Needs' based on Maslow's theory.

What I am giving you here is the Personality Recipe based on my interpretation of Maslow's work. A breakdown of what the key human personality ingredients are and how you can work out your precise mix of these which will result in a balanced and resourcefully created version of you.

Getting to grips with this recipe will give you clarity around your behaviour and emotions. You will see why you have some of the results you have and, if necessary, you can then make changes.

It also gives insight into other people's behaviour and you gain an understanding of why they do what they do. You can then empower them to respond differently and also empower yourself to respond differently to them or the situation. It gives you another perspective into how you operate.

The beauty of this personality recipe is that it is valid in all areas of your life: work, relationships, social interactions and personal interests, amongst other things. Once you see the patterns and what your unique personality recipe is, all areas of your life can be adjusted if necessary.

You will also have the tools to have a frank conversation with your nearest and dearest. If your behaviour is destructive to a relationship or vice versa, you can then find a solution together. You can begin to understand how they are interlinked and to meet each other's needs resourcefully.

If you're experiencing anxiety or mild depression, then understanding your key personality ingredients can give you a means to seeing a way forward and changing what you're currently doing.

Of all the people who have been given the blueprint to their personality recipe, every one of them has had an immediate insight into their behaviour and plenty of 'Aha' moments.

To not understand your emotional and spiritual needs and see how they influence your life is a bit like sticking your finger in your ears, shutting your eyes and going 'La la la' like a belligerent child.

Not gaining insight into your behaviour and your needs is to say that you don't care, not just about yourself, but also of those around you as your behaviour may impact them. You'll never have the ability to change or you'll struggle to change.

The Personality Recipe has six essential ingredients. Like all good recipes, they require the right balance of the essential ingredients: Stability, Diversity, Significance, Relationship and Bonds, Personal Development and Giving.

Just as our tastes in food vary and we adjust recipes to reflect these tastes, the same is true of our personality recipes. We test, adjust, taste and keep going until we have something that works.

> **Personality Ingredients**
> Stability
> Diversity
> Significance
> Relationships and Bonds
> Personal Development
> Giving

Like all ingredients you use, there are different options and these impact the end result. You might use tinned potatoes so the final taste and texture of your dish will be different to that of using fresh potatoes. The same is true with our personality recipes and the table below is an example of how the options you utilise impact your final results.

Personality Recipe

Personality Ingredients	Great Options	Dubious Options
Stability	• Backing self • Positive routines • Organisation • Certainty of self	• Controlling others • Constant TV-watching • Obsessive-compulsive behaviour • Procrastination • Boredom
Diversity	• Adventurous to new challenges • Social butterfly • Ability to reframe or create new meanings around events • Hobbies • Creativity	• Self-sabotage • Excessive drinking • Drug abuse • Easily overwhelmed • Unnecessarily creating drama

Significance	• Achieving goals • Leader of self and of others • Volunteering	• Gossiping • Lying for attention • Playing the victim • Putting others down • Rebellion
Relationships and Bonds	• Sharing and being supportive • Unconditional love • Connecting with nature • Self-love and self-worth	• Self-harm • Participating in needy and/or unhealthy relationships • Loneliness
Personal Development	• Lifelong learning	• Not taking action on learning
Giving	• Helping others • Volunteering • Donation to charity • Paying it forward	• Giving to get • Playing a martyr • Giving without care to self

What to Do: Step 1

Now that you have seen the Personality Recipe, how do you go about putting it together and getting your version right?

I'm guessing that when you looked at the ingredients list, you probably identified with one immediately. Actually, I think the others are also relevant. They all do come into play and some will be more dominant than others depending on the situation.

Look at the key ingredients and place them in an order that is most important to you. There is no right or wrong. It may be that two are equal in importance and that is fine. Comment as to why they are important and it is important to be clear. Once you have done this, then you can start the process of balancing out the flavours!

When I went to Peru on a charity trek, my ingredients of Significance and Diversity were met. My Significance was in doing something public and important. My Diversity was my need for adventure and travel. But they were also tempered by the need for Stability as I had a son at home who was going to be looked after by my husband. I needed to know that there were certain logistics in place that would ensure continuity in the home routine during my absence.

Through the experience I had, my needs for Personal Development and Giving were satisfied. I was learning and evolving and I was giving because it was a charity event. As you can see, most ingredients are involved.

What to Do: Step 2

The balance of all these personality ingredients will normally result in a balanced and happy person. But chances are that you're feeling out of whack, not happy at just being a mum and not fully understanding why. Your personality ingredients are not balanced and need a little adjustment so you need to look at the variation of ingredients you are using.

When our family moved out of London, we swapped a small cramped flat at a busy location for a larger house with a garden and a local village school for my son.

But I was really unhappy and I couldn't figure out why. I remember sitting down one day in tears and I said to my husband, 'I've got everything I wanted, but I don't feel happy.'

I chatted to the doctor who was insistent on prescribing me anti-depressants but I was resistant to that idea. Sure, I was down but I instinctively knew that I didn't need drugs to help pull me out of it. Eventually, I got through it but if I had known about the Personality Recipe, I would have come to my realisation much sooner.

I had given up a full-time job and was no longer working, my friends were not close by and all the facilities and resources I loved were no longer nearby. My need for significance was not being met at all at that point. I had lost my significance and also some of my relationships and bonds. I eventually worked my way through it and met my need for significance in a more constructive manner.

So, let's quickly get you to your personality recipe!

Examine the questions below. Anything below 6 is when you start to feel the pain and stress around the activity or situation. If you're feeling crappy about something, then you are probably using the ingredient incorrectly.

Your key to working this out is your behaviour. For example, do you spend more than necessary on material things? If so, you're probably trying to gain significance by doing this. Likewise, gossiping meets the need for significance. Do you spend lots of time in front of the television? Is it a constructive way of meeting stability through routine?

- What is something that you currently do, that you enjoy doing and are motivated to do?

- Go through the six personality ingredients. Evaluate how much that activity fulfils those ingredients on a scale of 1–10 (with 10 meaning this activity totally fulfils this need).

- What activity do you currently struggle to do, something you know you 'should' do but never feel an inner drive to actually complete it?

- Rate how well that activity fulfils your six personality ingredients.

You will find that the activities you struggle to complete are those that don't fulfil at least one of your personality ingredients. They will be below 6 out of 10.

What to Do: Step 3

It's great that you've stuck your hand up and admitted there are aspects of your personality that probably needs some work. The good news is that you have complete control over how you behave and now that you are recognising the less positive aspects, you can deal with them. Just as you can adjust the type or quantity of ingredients when a recipe doesn't turn out the way you want, you can tweak your personality recipe.

Using the questions in Step 2, you can evaluate key areas of your life. How does your family meet your needs? How does your current financial situation meet your needs? What do you do in your spare time? How does that meet your needs?

Then look at the aspects that are not meeting your needs and look at how you can adjust the balance. In other words, what can you change to create the perfect recipe?

So, if your top ingredient is Diversity but this is not being met within your family life, then look at what you can introduce to change it up.

Perhaps you can sign up for a class that interests you. A frank conversation with your partner explaining how you feel can give way to more understanding and potential solutions since you are talking and taking ownership rather than nagging or shouting. See how this can generate change and balance?

You may experience resistance to change, especially if it feels like it's a personal dig at how you're behaving but, remember, all this is about is changing a familiar recipe and making it better.

Nice Try but I've Heard It Before

Sometimes, my clients react by throwing their hands up in horror and thinking that they can never watch television again! But it's about balance. I am partial to vegging out and watching TV or DVDs. It's a time for me to switch off and that's fine.

I'm not saying don't ever watch TV but be aware of what is productive. A couple of hours here and there are cool but when it becomes your constant companion and routine, then it's time to question what this is replacing.

A far more constructive routine for me is a daily walk, which meets my need for stability and is a far healthier way than sitting on the sofa all evening.

I often get asked if the Personality Recipe is the answer to depression. If you think you are suffering from depression or anxiety, I would, without question, urge you to seek medical advice in the first instance to get a clear diagnosis. If you are currently on medication, do not come off of it without medical advice.

Personally, I think any tool or exercise that enables us to understand our thinking and emotions is empowering and can be used in conjunction with other prescribed medication or therapies.

Another thing which crops up is that people say that it seems too simple. Absolutely, it is simple and that's the beauty. You don't have to spend untold amounts of time trying to wade through psychology theory just to get to the point of understanding something that will assist in propelling you forward.

A human being needs food, water, sleep and exercise to function physiologically but we don't need to know all the biological theory behind it. The same is with our emotions. If we have the basic knowledge that enables us to take action and change, then why get bogged down with the theory? You're more likely to yawn and put this book down if I included more theoretical explanations, so get those valuable sleeps-ins!

Your Key Actions and Learnings

1. Identify in what order of importance the personality ingredients are to you.

2. Look at the key areas in your life and assess how these are meeting your personality ingredients. Are your options working for you?

3. Assess what needs to be adjusted and look at how you can achieve this.

It is impossible to live without failing at something, unless you live so cautiously that you might as well not have lived at all – in which case, you fail by default.

J.K. Rowling

5. Pick Yourself Up and Dust Yourself Down
– *There's No Such Thing as Failure, Only Feedback*

Let's cut to the chase: you are going to fall down, you are going to stuff up but you sure as hell are going to get back up and try again. The sooner you get over this one, the better. There will be times when you get things right the first time and times when you don't. It's how life rock and rolls. You don't expect your children to get it right the first time so why have that expectation of yourself?

Always remember that every time you make a mistake, you're one step closer to getting it right. So stop seeing things that don't work as failures and see them as opportunities to grow. See them as feedback on what you can do to get it right.

Not getting things right means this is an opportunity to learn, change and grow.

Your project or idea may need a tweak or a major change, or it could be that you need to move onto something else to get your outcome but there is always a lesson you can draw from it.

If you are in a situation where things haven't gone to plan and if it's a recurring theme, then use this to assess your thinking. You might have beliefs that are holding you back from doing things the right way. Pause and take time to look at what you believe and change the belief. Your behaviour changes and you may start getting things right.

You become more flexible in your behaviour as you learn to adapt until you get it right. After a while, you learn to problem solve much quicker. Not seeing things as failures opens you up to more possibilities if you know that you cannot fail. You will be more willing to try different things. There is often a 'failure' side to every success story. Those who are successful keep trying.

If you constantly tell yourself that you failed, you're creating beliefs to support that. You're giving yourself stories about what you can't do and this will stop you from trying anything again or experiencing different things. You'll stay with what's familiar. You'll never evolve into a better version of yourself or create the life and passions that you desire.

To sum it up in a nutshell, there's no such thing as failure, only feedback. And by failure, I mean to assume that someone is not succeeding in achieving their desired outcome. On the other hand, feedback is information given and received in order to enhance or improve a product or performance. Spot the difference?

What to Do: Step 1

Scrap the word 'failure' from your vocabulary. It should no longer exist and here's how to move forward differently.

Get used to asking for and accepting feedback. It's not personal criticism, it's about seeking an opportunity for you to improve, a chance to hear what works well and what doesn't.

Also, not only will you get to know exactly what you're doing right and what needs to be adjusted, you're giving others an opportunity to have a voice and be part of the process. You are acknowledging and giving value to others' opinion or expertise. It's a gift for you and a gift for them!

As a child minder in the UK, one has to be assessed by OFSTED, a regulatory body that oversees the education of children. They review all schools, child centres and home-care practices. Their inspections are compulsory.

I got through my first inspection satisfactorily which, given that I had only been in the business for a few weeks, was a good start. The feedback allowed me to know what I was doing well and what I needed to change. This helped me to be better. At the end of the day, it was about being the best that I could be in providing the service to my clients.

It was only the small things that I had missed and they were easy to adjust but it gave me a benchmark to aim for. If you come off the starting block as an expert, how are you ever going to grow? No one is ever an expert in absolutely everything but knowing that you can improve gives you the momentum to constantly seek improvement in what you're choosing to do or deliver.

What to Do: Step 2

Next, you need to learn to listen to yourself more or, in other words, do as you say to others! Think of all the times your children have tried something and not got it right the first time. They get a bit despondent, don't want to try again or might get upset. What have you told them? Have you helped them and encouraged them? I'm betting that you are pretty positive, supportive and encouraging.

Now, start telling yourself the same things because I bet that you're not going to turn around to your children and say, 'Oh, you're no good, you're useless, don't bother and give up now.' If you don't tell your children that, then why would you tell yourself that? Just because we're adults doesn't mean we should change our expectations and assume that everything goes well the first time.

I frequently say to my children that when something doesn't go quite the way they had hoped, it doesn't matter as long as they have learnt from that. I always get them to tell me what it is that they have learnt. When I get a little frustrated at an outcome, I remind myself of what I say to my children and turn it around into what I could have done better or differently.

Think of key things you say to friends and family when you feel that they've not been successful. Remind yourself that you wouldn't talk to others the way you talk to yourself, so start being nicer and kinder to yourself and stop the negative self-talk.

Look at the positives in all the situations that you had previously regarded as failures. It can be something really small or things that are big. Just start to look for alternative solutions.

What to Do: Step 3

Finally, look back on your life experiences. How many times have you got things wrong or things didn't go to plan and you didn't stop to think about it? You just picked yourself up and carried on.

What were you actually telling yourself at the time? Why did you decide to carry on? Remind yourself of what you did and use that to encourage yourself in times when you have self-doubt. Remember that no matter how bad things might have seemed at the time, you didn't explode into flames!

In the early days of my jewellery business, I did all my practice designs using silver, which was expensive. One day, nothing was going right. Everything I tried just didn't have the right feel to it. I looked at all the silver I had wasted and I was really annoyed and frustrated.

After having a minor tantrum, I calmed down and looked at it rationally. I then found alternative materials that I could use for mock-up designs which didn't cost so much if I'd got it wrong. I then had the confidence to be more creative because it wasn't going to cost lots of money if I stuffed it up.

I now also keep all my 'mistakes' because I can melt them at a later date and create something else out of my mistakes! Problem solved. I didn't fail, I just needed to rethink how I was going to go about doing it.

I like you to jot down the times you found solutions to situations and carried on regardless until you got the results you wanted. Make a note of what you did, what you told yourself and what your motivation to continue was. In doing so, you are building up that resource list for times when you're struggling and can refer to it.

Nice Try but I've Heard It Before

I've come across people who have the mindset that they fail at everything. That is not quite true. Most things we do were unfamiliar at some point. We just try again if it doesn't work out. Some people focus on what they haven't achieved or 'failed' at but do not acknowledge their successes. It also might be that you're trying things that you don't really want to do or have some negative beliefs around your ability.

Examine what you're doing that you feel is going wrong all the time. Is it something you really want to be doing or something you think you 'should' be doing? What are your beliefs around trying something new? Are you telling yourself that new things are always difficult?

Sometimes, people get put off by external criticism when they're trying something new and I always say, 'That's about them, not you.' They're feeling insecure about something and choosing to reflect it on you. Bat it back, smile and thank them for their attention and say that you would appreciate their feedback on how to do it differently. I guarantee you that it will make them pause and take responsibility for their words and behaviour.

Another question I get is, 'How many times can I fail before it's ok to give up?' Firstly, there is no failure. The question I would ask is, 'How many times do I need to keep trying to succeed?' And you will always keep trying to succeed because once you've achieved something you move onto the next level and so on. It's a constant flow forward. It's like being a mum. You'll always be a mum and you'll never stop learning how to be a mum. The challenges thrown at you are just different as your children grow.

Your Key Actions and Learnings

1. Jot down in a journal the times you have found solutions to situations and carried on until you got the results you wanted.

2. Think of the key things you say to friends and family when they feel they have not been successful. Keep them in a journal for you to refer to when you need a pep talk!

3. Look for positives in all situations especially those that you previously regarded as 'failures'.

What you hope for, you also fear.

Alice Walker

6. Hiring the Right Home Help
– *Facing Your Fears*

I don't know about you but I have a constant conversation going on in my head which sometimes turns into a comical argument. 'Yes, you can' followed by 'No, you can't'. I'm sure you've seen the cartoons depicting this: a devil on one shoulder and an angel on the other. I actually have names for mine: the devil is Mini-me and the angel is Big Me.

Fear, if you allow it to win, is your biggest enemy. Both those voices have the same intent. They both want to serve you. However, one wants to keep you safe, to not take chances nor try different things and the other one wants to progress.

You need to learn to listen to the right voice. Learning to embrace fear is a normal part of life. It means you learn to push past that sense of fear and to move forward. Normally, that fear means you're on the edge of making change.

Remember when you were a child and you did the school play. You had those butterflies in your stomach but you had no choice. You had to get on that stage and perform. Before you know it, you were in front of an audience and you had finished the play. Everyone applauded you and you exited the stage, saying to yourself, *Actually, that wasn't too bad, I got through it.* And in the following year, you had the confidence to put yourself up for a bigger part.

Fear is also a flashing light. It's an indicator that you may need to change your thinking. In other words, question and analyse what you're afraid of. Is it a genuine fear or something else underlying that? Chances are that it's not a response to a situation that requires you to run, as if from a house fire, but more of a personal fear such as a fear of failure. This is something you can have control over and deal with.

Learning to deal with fear resourcefully is like giving a gift to your family. They can learn from your examples. If you can confront your fear and still go through to complete your goals, then your children are going to model this behaviour.

Learning and having the strategies to manage your fears are things that you can pass onto others. There's no bigger gift than teaching a child not to be afraid.

How many times have we told our children not to worry, that there is nothing to be scared of and then explained the reasons why they shouldn't be scared? Children will model on what you demonstrate.

Anyone remember the monster under the bed, the first day at school or our first sports day? Remember how our parents taught us that everything was going to be fine and, for the most part, it was? So try saying that to yourself and believe it!

The more you push past your fears and do what needs to be done anyway, the more evidence you have to know that you can do it again and again. You think back to that time and say, *Crikey, I was so scared about doing that new evening class but it wasn't that bad. People weren't scary and I made new friends.* And so you have that knowledge as your benchmark in the future.

The 'doing' then becomes easier and your confidence to deal with fear will grow. You also realise that if things don't go exactly as planned, it doesn't matter. You develop the resources to deal with them. In other words, you start off dealing with low-quality problems and then move up to dealing with high-quality problems.

Remember that little child doing the school play who just had a small part and they conquered that fear of going on stage. That was their small problem. The next year, they were going for the main part. So the higher quality problem becomes, *How do I remember all my lines?* and so on.

Generally, fear is the biggest reason why women who were successful before having children now struggle to make sense of their current world since a world that used to make sense no longer exists. There is a fear about their lost abilities. There are questions regarding their capability to move forward and a sense of being stuck between two worlds.

Not learning to deal with fear effectively and accepting it as a normal part of life means that you won't evolve, grow and create change. You'll learn to live with regret and remain stuck. Perhaps two, three or five years will pass and, the next thing you know, your children have left home. You look back on your life and think, *Why didn't I do that? I could have done this but I didn't.*

What to Do: Step 1

Sometimes, fear may not be obvious. You might be giving yourself excuses for not doing things such as 'I haven't got the time' or you may be procrastinating by saying that you cannot manage XYZ. Those are disguises for fear.

Before you start huffing and puffing at the above statement believing that you can legitimise all the reasons you put forward for not doing something – and I know, you think they are genuine – have a real good look at what you are really saying by putting it in the following context.

Behind every excuse – or use the word 'reason' if that makes you feel better – is the fear of:

    A. not being loved

    B. not being good enough

    C. failure.

It could be that you don't really want to do it anyway; in which case, just admit it and ditch it! Once you know the fear underlying your lack of action, then you can figure out the 'why' of the fear and 'how' you can combat this.

When the Parent-Teacher Association (PTA) was looking for volunteers and I was thinking whether to do it or not, I had this mad conversation going on in my head. Big Me was saying, *Just do it, just do it*. Mini-me was saying, *No, no, you won't be able to do it. You don't know the area, you don't know the people. How can you help out? You've only been here three weeks. What can you contribute?* I could have thought of a multitude of 'reasons' to not do it but, deep down, I knew it was really about the fear of failing and not being good enough.

Luckily, my Big Me won over and I just did it. Did I do a fantastic job? Probably not. But I did it and I gave it a go and I achieved quite a few things with the help of other people on the committee. I now know that I can do it so I continue to put my hand up to do things I haven't done before.

Recently, I stuck my hand up to be the team manager for my daughter's soccer club. I haven't got a clue about soccer rules but no one wanted the job and I thought, *Hey, I've got this, I've been here before and I know I can do it.* I had my evidence for knowing that I can handle what I don't know.

Next time you start having that negative self-talk, pause for a moment to think. What is it really about? Is it the fear of failing? Is it the fear of not being good enough? Or not being loved?

Once you've identified this, you can look for the evidence to support yourself and for the strategies to overcome this. Before I joined the PTA, I was telling myself that I was going to fail because I didn't know anyone in the area. But I countered that by thinking, *Well, it's a committee of several people so I can go to them for help. I don't have to go it alone.*

Think about something that you have achieved which you were scared about but did it anyway. What did you tell yourself? What did you allow yourself to hear? How did you learn and grow from this? By changing your self-talk, you can talk yourself into it rather than out of it.

You can embrace uncertainty, knowing that you have the strategies in place to deal with it.

What to Do: Step 2

Next, I would advise you to practice, practice, practice. When an opportunity comes up, say Yes immediately. Don't have that head conversation. Commit to it. Trust that you can do it, that you will find the necessary resources to rise to the challenge. Embrace the fear and learn to see setbacks as another step forward toward excellence and expertise. The more you face up to fear, the easier it becomes.

Many years ago, I became a party plan consultant for a big cosmetics company in the UK. When it came to my very first party, I felt sick with fear and thought, *I don't know anyone, what am I going to do? What if I don't sell anything? What if I forget the product knowledge?*

When I got to the hostess's house, there wasn't a table which I wasn't prepared for. This added to the anxiety I was already feeling. We actually ended up using an ironing board to display products on but I got through it. I got sales, I managed to remember most of what I needed to (and what I didn't know, the audience was probably not aware). I learnt from it and got through it without bursting into flames! I continued, I progressed and I got better.

When I came to Australia, I was a party plan consultant for another skincare and cosmetics company. Since I learnt to deal with the fear, it wasn't such a big thing for me as I was familiar with going into strange houses, to expect the unexpected and having an audience to demonstrate to. Having that confidence to embrace uncertainty helped me to achieve top sales in my first month of consulting and I only ran two parties. I did not see that possibility at my first demonstration!

I learnt that fear wasn't to be feared, that I could get through it. Any situation that came up, I knew that I had the skillset to deal with it.

What to Do: Step 3

Fear is something we've learnt to feel. Look at young kids: they don't know failure and fear. Watch a young toddler learning to walk. They take their first steps and fall over.

But they don't sit on their bum and say, *That's it. That hurt, I'm not going to do it anymore.* They keep on doing it, falling over and picking themselves up until they learn to walk.

Fear isn't in their mindset or in their vocabulary. It's something they learn through us saying, 'Oh, don't do that, you'll hurt yourself' or 'Be careful ...' and so on. They hear the language that teaches them fear.

So, given that we can teach an old dog new tricks, we can learn to not have fear in our vocabulary or change our mindset around it. We can give it a new name.

It doesn't have to be 'fear', it could be 'this is unfamiliar to me' or 'this is unknown to me'. We can think differently. How about believing that fear means you are on the brink of something exciting? Imagine what possibilities are open to you now.

Nice Try but I've Heard It Before

For some, it can be hard to let go of that security blanket of excuses and claim that things will never work out, that there are always obstacles. 'There's no one to babysit so if I cannot go out and try new things, then what's the point in trying?'

Well, that's called life. It's never smooth. How many obstacles and problems come up in a day that you unconsciously solve? You will be surprised at how many solutions you come up with on any given day. There is always a solution. You just need to choose to find it.

Another thing that people tend to focus on is what hasn't gone according to plan. 'The last time I tried something, it was a disaster. Nothing went right.'

Really? Nothing went right? Absolutely everything you did was a disaster? You didn't manage to get to the venue on time? Did the booking go through? Did you find the materials? What's your definition of disaster? Was it more about you feeling uncomfortable? There would have been things that did go well, so use the experience to learn and do it differently next time.

I love it when people throw in the argument, 'But fear protects us from danger.' Yes, fear is for more rational situations like if your house is on fire, then get out but, as I mentioned earlier, most fears are irrational which we're taught through experience and language.

Irrational fears have no dangerous consequences when you put yourself in that situation, so there is a clear difference between a genuinely dangerous situation which is potentially life threatening and an irrational fear. Learn to tell the difference between the two.

Your Key Actions and Learnings

Now that we know your excuses for procrastination are actually based on fear and insecurity, there are three actions that I would like you to do.

1. Listen to your self-talk and identify the fears.

2. Embrace your fear. Keep doing it and develop positive strategies.

3. Fear is an invention so invent something new.

Recommended reading: *Feel the Fear and Do It Anyway* by Susan Jeffers.

The best way to treat obstacles is to use them as stepping stones. Laugh at them, tread on them, and let them lead you to something better.

Enid Blyton, *Mr Galliano's Circus*

7. Yoga for the Mind

– *Learning to be Flexible*

Creating change is not always a straight path and you have to learn to adapt and be flexible. Chances are that you're going to find obstacles along your journey.

Mothers are fantastic at being flexible. It becomes second nature as things are constantly changing, especially in those early years of raising children.

Hands up those who felt relief at finally working out a nap routine and organising things around that but then a few weeks later it all changes and things. Things have to be re-organised again! After a while, the constant change becomes a familiar pattern and you just get on with it.

Clients often come to me about creating change in their lives. They seem to forget that they have the ability to be flexible despite the fact they do it on a daily basis. They cite all the reasons why they cannot do something because they only see the obstacles.

To see an obstacle is often a way of dealing with fear because it legitimises and gives you a reason to not do something. However, the more you practice being resourceful and flexible, the more likely those fears will disappear. Obstacles then become opportunities which grow your ability to think outside the box.

As you learn to be flexible when dealing with obstacles, you create a positive mindset; instead of giving up, it becomes a challenge. And the more challenges you meet, the more confident you are in finding solutions. It's about building a muscle which may not have been used that much before. The ability to adapt is the ability to complete.

When I discuss obstacles, I'm not talking about a physical obstacle but an objection, an excuse or a perceived reason for not doing something, such as, 'I cannot afford that course' or 'I don't have the time to commit to writing that story.'

As you build that flexibility muscle, you become more tolerant and accepting of life in general. Instead of being reactive, you become more proactive so obstacles become less drama-driven which in turn makes you calmer. The calmer you are, the more likely you are able to find a great solution and feel in control of the situation rather than the situation controlling you.

This also gives others a confidence in your ability to tackle projects so they may offer you opportunities. You become the go-to person because they know that you have the flexibility and attitude to adapt to situations. Following that, you get to deal with the (high-quality) problems that you want rather than the small problems which are just going to niggle you and not serve any purpose.

Getting fit and building muscles can be challenging but if you don't learn to build that flexibility muscle and have a flexible mindset, then you're going to constantly feel as if you're hitting that proverbial wall.

Everything becomes a problem and you fail to see solutions so you never go further than where you are currently at. You may become resentful and see the world as being against you rather than with you. That also has a knock-on effect on your family life and on those around you. If everything is a problem, then you become this person who constantly moans about how everything goes wrong or how nothing goes your way. People will simply not want to be around you.

You know you can do it. By being a mother, you have proven time and time again that you have the ability to be flexible. Use it to turn things around for what you want.

What to Do: Step 1

Grab those leg warmers and leotards and let's get flexible.

Be absolutely clear on your vision, see your bigger picture and then plan out what you need to do to get there. That way, you can see the potential issues and work out the solutions.

Think of it as a jigsaw puzzle. You have the box, the finished picture on the lid and inside are the pieces you need. You need to make sense of that pile and put them together. It's a bit like those ideas floating around in your brain. You need to make sense of them. So, you get all the straight edges and make the frame. That's the structure. You spot other pieces and fit them together. You work with these so you get familiar and then you get some more pieces, adding to the jigsaw.

In the end, you have a complete picture; in other words, your end goal or vision. You then realise that it was possible and you move from doing a 1000-piece jigsaw to a 1500-piece jigsaw.

Get your ideas down on paper or whatever way it works for you. Use lists, mind maps (a pictorial representation comprising of a central idea linked to other words, items and concepts), coloured pens and pictures. Then, as much as you are able to, put in all the things you may need to work towards your goal.

In January, I sit down and do my yearly goal setting. I break my big visions down into sections such as work goals, health goals and family goals and then do mind maps for each section. This forms my big picture.

I then break it down into quarterly goals with the corresponding month-by-month steps. That way, I have a clear plan and a structure. I use coloured pens, mind maps and then write it all down into positive statements. The process of writing helps cement it.

I never look further than the quarter I am in so I don't get overwhelmed. You can tweak things if needed. There is no point in following something religiously if it's not delivering the results you need.

What to Do: Step 2

Sometimes, being flexible and finding solutions means compromising and you may have to find alternatives to your game plan. Let's be clear, compromising is not a precursor to giving up or that you have to wait for the right moment. It's about finding solutions.

I hate to break it to you but there is never going to be an ideal time. The planets are never going to align. You have to work with the here-and-now. You can always find a reason for not doing something so start finding the way to do something.

What can you do to move towards your goal in the situation you're in now? Not the situation that you think you're going to be in a week's time or a month's time or in a year's time – what can you do now with what you have?

As soon as you realise that you have to do it now, you will deal with that obstacle as it is. Taking that action will move you forward to create the moment. Face it: you never know what's in store. Life has a way of throwing curve balls that you cannot predict.

Just say Yes to what it is you want to do and the 'how' will work itself out. There have been many occasions when I have seized the moment and said Yes to an opportunity without the slightest idea of how I was going to make it work. But I always found the solution. Conversely, the opportunities that I have not grasped immediately and said, 'I would think about it' have ended up as missed opportunities.

There has rarely been a perfect time for when I have done things. When I decided to go to university, the course I wanted to do was miles away so travelling costs were high. I was giving up work so I lost income but I still had a flat to pay for. It was not ideal but I figured that I would make it work. I learnt to ride a motorbike – an adolescent dream achieved although after some cold and wet months of riding, the shine wore off! – so I saved on the train fares.

My banking background ensured that I got highly paid temp jobs in the holidays and I did some cleaning jobs during the term. I made it work with what I had at the time which was just as well since I fell pregnant with my son towards the end of my degree. Had I waited for the planets to align, I probably would never have started and completed my course!

What to Do: Step 3

The third thing I would advise is practice, practice, practice and consistently build that flexibility muscle. If you're frustrated with a situation or an outcome which you weren't expecting, instead of moaning about it, think of a positive alternative. For example, you might be in the doctor's surgery and they're running late with appointments. Instead of feeling frustrated and having that self-talk about what you 'could' be doing, try doing something that you can do there and then, such as jotting down notes for a project.

Try to see the positive in the situation. You now have some time to catch up with a friend on your mobile phone or to start reading a book. If a friend cancels on you at the last minute for a night out, then go out and see a movie. Light some candles and have a relaxing bath with a glass of wine or bulk cook for the week. Do whatever floats your boat.

Use positive language. Change 'I can't' to 'How can I …?' or 'It's not possible' to 'What's going to make it possible?' Feel and hear the power changing just by tweaking a couple of words.

Nice Try but I've Heard It Before

'Yeah but my obstacles are genuine,' I hear you say. 'I really don't have the time, money and <insert your excuse here>.' And so are everyone else's. How you choose to deal with the perceived obstacles is your choice and you have complete control over that. You lack time? Spend a day cooking and make the next month's meals. Voila! Free time. Lack money for a venture? Can you share the costs with a friend? There are always solutions.

'I am who I am so why change the way I think' is a classic response, normally accompanied with a big pout. Nothing ever remains the same. Do you respond to situations today in the same way you did ten years ago or when you were a teenager? I doubt it.

Learning behavioural flexibility is a muscle that needs constant exercise. I suggest you ask yourself what you are really 'stuck' with. I can almost guarantee that it's not about obstacles but more around a fear.

Sometimes, people state that things are out of their control. They perceive that as being a legitimate obstacle to their goals. Sure, things do happen that we cannot control but we are always in control of how we respond to others and situations. Sorry, there is no legitimate excuse to be had there!

Your Key Actions and Learnings

1. Be clear on your vision. Brainstorm and get your ideas down on paper.

2. Be prepared to trade off in the beginning.

3. Practice being flexible and being adaptable.

Accepting help is its own kind of strength.

Kiera Cass

8. Picking Your Team

– *Knowing When to Get Help*

The word 'help' can bring about all sorts of negative thoughts such as 'I'm being weak', 'I can't cope', 'I'm not managing' or 'I'm not good enough'. But my way of thinking is that seeking help is a strength. It's the ability to recognise that things get achieved far better by utilising other resources and teamwork. As the saying goes, no man (woman) is an island!

If people are willing to help and it's going to get you there faster, then why wouldn't you want it? Getting help from those who know more, who are experts and can fill the gaps of knowledge that you do not have means that you start to become an expert.

We don't know everything about everything and if you decide to focus and develop a particular interest or project, then find out as much as possible. So look to someone who knows more than you to help. And it's not just about getting help with knowledge but also getting practical help to free you up.

If you've got children, then who can you get onboard to look after them for a while? Have you got relatives? Have you got friends? Do you get a child minder? Do you put them into a day-care setting for a few hours? That's still help but of a practical nature.

Getting help can avoid other problems down the line. For example, chat to an accountant about what you need to set up for a microbusiness so that you're compliant with the tax laws. The last thing you want is to find out that you've been doing the wrong thing and get a fine. Or it might be that specific tools and materials are required. By talking to an expert to find out what you're going to need versus what is nice to have, you can avoid expensive and unnecessary mistakes in your purchases.

Is it really worth reinventing the wheel? If it's been done before and has been done well, then focus on the things that can be different. In other words, make use of your uniqueness, creativity and points of difference.

Take writing this book as an example. There is a certain order of procedures to get it to the physical product which you are currently holding. I could (eventually) work out how to create a cover, learn a graphics package, obtain an ISBN and so on. But there are experts out there who have the contacts, knowledge and expertise. They can cut out months of work and frustration for me, leaving me to do the creative bit, that is, the content which will make this book unique.

Recent research has shown that most people underestimate the power of asking for help.[1] They assume that more people will say No rather than Yes. Yet, the opposite is true.

1   Flynn, Francis J. and Lake, Vanessa K. B., 'If You Need Help, Just Ask: Underestimating Compliance With Direct Requests for Help', *Journal of Personality and Social Psychology*, Vol. 95, No. 1, 2008, pp. 128–143.

More people actually say Yes to your request for help than expected. There're a lot of people willing to help who are not being asked!

Your world won't fall apart if you ask for help. If you don't ask for help when it's needed, then it can result in you repeating the same mistakes and not knowing why or not even realising that you're making them. It will take you longer to realise your ambitions or, worse still, you may not realise them at all. It will compound and perpetuate feelings of helplessness because you are not feeling any sense of achievement.

Let me reiterate that asking for help is a positive, not a negative. Help is about seeking assistance of an advisory or a practical nature which enables you to solve, focus or address areas that you may not have full knowledge about or the means to move forward in your chosen venture or idea.

What to Do: Step 1

What are great steps towards getting help?

Firstly, utilise good friends. People like to feel valued. Seeking advice or an opinion or help does that as you are acknowledging their value and as someone who you can trust.

People are generally happy to be a sounding board. When people have come to me for help, they say, 'Oh my God, sorry, I've just offloaded on you.' I always answer that it is far easier listening to and helping out with someone else's problems than dealing with my own. I am sure that you have probably thought something similar.

Also, chatting to people may give you a different perspective. It's a good way to get out of your own head. I have a couple of go-to friends who seem to magically and instantly have solutions to things that I've been stewing about. Within five minutes of listening to me, they say, 'Have you thought about or do you realise …?' It's sort of a 'Duh' moment when I slap my hand on my forehead and think, *Ah, of course, the answer was staring me right in the face!*

If you've got friends like that who are able to give you a different perspective, to give you a bit of a push, then use them as a sounding board. And if they call you out on your behaviour, take it onboard as constructive feedback. You might not always like being told what you're doing isn't great but, once you've absorbed the words and have stepped away from it, it can be the most useful thing that a good friend does for you.

Remember to reciprocate their help when they need it. Don't become the person they want to avoid because you drain them of their energy and just take all the time. Look at the people who you go to for solutions and model them. What is it that they do that you don't? What strategies do they utilise? What attitude do they adopt? What useful things do they tell themselves in moments of adversity? The more you can model positive behaviours and mindsets, the more productive you will be.

What to Do: Step 2

Secondly, unless you're conducting a financial transaction – that is, paying an agreed amount for a specific service or goods – always go in with a 'What can I contribute?' attitude.

In other words, what can you do for the person who is helping you? Don't just take from the person. You need to be able to give back too. It doesn't have to be immediately but make sure you keep that little mental tally. It could be a bottle of wine, an exchange of labour or a thank-you note. If they have a business, then maybe give out recommendations.

Always be open to help others even if you do not need help from them yet. You never know when you may need them.

If you build a reputation of being someone that is always willing to help, others will in turn want to help you.

When I was backpacking and was working as a casual for a department store in Sydney, I worked in ladies' shoes. A customer came in who was in her 60s and she had a real problem finding stylish shoes that fitted due to her arthritis. She had a wardrobe full of shoes which looked stylish but didn't really feel comfortable so she didn't wear them.

I was determined that this customer was going to leave with shoes that fitted her requirements. I spent about one and a half hours with her until we found a pair that she really liked and were comfortable with. She was really pleased and, as far as I was concerned, that was the end of that.

In fact, she happened to be a very close friend of the store manager and relayed how much time and help I had given her so that when I wanted to travel, I was guaranteed a position back at the store once I came back. You never know how being helpful to others can actually turn out to be a benefit down the line.

What to Do: Step 3

Thirdly, know what it is you want and be specific. Don't sit and moan to a friend and hint and hope that they understand what you're saying. We are not all mind-readers but we can tell when we are being primed for help! Spell it out. If you want to go to a painting class, then say, 'I found this great class and I'm looking for someone to look after my son on a Tuesday from 6 to 8 pm. Are you able to have him at that time?'

Honing down on the specifics can also make what you need more manageable to others. 'I have no help for the evening' is ambiguous and can sound like a huge request whereas 'I need help for two hours' is a specific and manageable request.

That way, the other person is clear on what you need. If they are not able to help, then they have the details to think of other options. Being vague rarely leads to the desired outcome.

When I was looking for a graphic designer to do my logo, my brief was clear. Having those specifics meant that I ruled out one designer because they couldn't meet my timeline. My second call wouldn't take on the brief because it wasn't their specialised area but they gave me a number of someone who could. Being specific lead me to getting what I wanted a lot quicker.

Nice Try but I've Heard It Before

I have come across people who are adamant that they have never asked for help and are not going to start now. I always challenge them by asking how they learned to tie their shoelaces. Gets them every time! My aim isn't to embarrass but to illustrate that, at some point in our lives, we have had help to learn, grow and achieve. It does not mean we are inadequate.

Some people love a challenge and don't see the benefits of getting help. I totally get that but I would advise to be wise about your choices. Know when it has a clear purpose and will be productive. For example, if you want a website and are tight on money and time, then let an expert do the backend and you write the content or vice versa depending on your strengths.

A lot of women don't like to ask for help because they fear being a burden on others. However, as I mentioned before, most people are happy to help. If they cannot directly help, then they will often help with finding a solution.

If you knew someone who was struggling, then what would you say to them? Chances are that you would offer to help and not consider it a burden. Think of it as giving a gift. You are showing them that you trust and value them.

> **Your Key Actions and Learnings**
>
> 1. Clarify the areas you need help with and make an action plan. Be specific about what you need and who to go to.
>
> 2. Look for opportunities to give value or help to others. It could be school reading, babysitting or inviting a new mum out for a coffee.
>
> 3. Start building your own resource and contacts file. What skill sets do other parents have? What professionals have been recommended to you? What contacts do you have from your professional work?

I wondered how many people there were in the world who suffered, and continued to suffer, because they could not break out from their own web of shyness and reserve, and in their blindness and folly built up a great distorted wall in front of them that hid the truth.

Daphne du Maurier, *Rebecca*

9. Adult Conversations

– The Value of Networking

One of the most important skills in life is the ability to network and to nurture relationships. As mothers, we often find the sort of conversations we're having not as stimulating and fulfilling as the ones we had when we were in the paid-working world.

However, it's important not to dismiss that connection with people or to think that there is nothing out there for you. The power of networking and being open to all sorts of conversations can lead to opportunities on so many levels.

Utilise what you have access to, even the school playground or during after-school activities. Continuing to build those connections not only keeps you stimulated but also helps you get out of your negative head space.

How many times have you sat at home with all that negative self-talk looping in your head thinking, *Gosh, I must be the only one who's experiencing this, feeling this or behaving like this.* By having conversations with other mums, you get the knowledge of other people saying, 'Yes, I know exactly what you mean.' You may be surprised at how many people have had similar experiences and it can be reassuring to know you are not going mad!

You may also open yourself up to new opportunities. Perhaps you mention that you are looking for new opportunities to start up a small business during a random conversation with a group in the playground. Someone may say, 'Yeah, I know someone who can help you with that.' You don't know what or who other people know until you talk to them.

The more you talk to people and engage them, the more opportunities you will find to try new skills. People might be discussing a new boxing class and ask you to join in. Before you know it, you're trying a new exercise class that you may not have felt comfortable doing on your own. But because you're going with someone else, you have the confidence to give it a go. This leads to excitement and you gain the confidence to try something else.

Networking also adds to your sense of contribution. By talking to other people, you're going to get involved in other things. It might be the PTA, it might be helping out a cake stall and that sense of belonging to a community through your network is invaluable. It gives you a sense of self-worth. The more others see you contributing, the more people remember you and want to connect with you.

All those skillsets which you learnt in the corporate world and fear losing because you are no longer using them outside of the workplace, such as, time management, negotiation skills, behavioural management, typing and report analysis, they all come into play when organising a school fete or event. You don't need to become rusty on your skillsets!

Got copywriting skills? Offer to do the school newsletter. Got events management experience? Organise a fundraiser. Are you a graphic designer? Help out with stage props for school performances. Starting to get the picture? Get involved and put yourself out there.

It may feel awkward. You may feel like you have nothing in common with the other mums. But the more you do it, the more likely you are going to meet people who interest you, make fantastic connections with and contribute to your community. You step into a world outside of your family life. And your kids will adore you for being involved!

In my experience, not networking and connecting with people can lead to anxiety and depression. You become lonely, isolated and unfulfilled. You start to behave destructively, even if it's mildly, like overeating, overspending, not exercising and feeling angry. You might resent people because you're assuming their life is better than yours. You have those negative, self-doubting voices constantly going around in your head which becomes a vicious cycle that you can't step out of.

Many people assume 'networking' is something you do in the corporate world but it isn't exclusive to that setting. Networking is about making connections with other people in any situation. It can be a brief exchange of words or a deep conversation. It requires the mutual engagement of two or more people reciprocating an interest in each other.

The process of networking helps us to be creative by stimulating new thoughts and ideas. Thus, it enhances our own internal connections to formulate a bigger picture of our lives. Furthermore, networking increases confidence. Who wouldn't want that?

What to Do: Step 1

How does one get started?

Firstly, utilise what you already have access to. You may be surprised at how much that actually is. Don't dismiss anything. I have had many constructive and enterprising conversations in the playground or even queues at the bank!

Be open to and look for opportunities to instigate a casual conversation and, most importantly, make the conversation about them and not you. Ask how their day is going, comment on a piece of clothing or jewellery you like. Don't expect to come away with anything. Go in with the mindset of what you can do for this person.

Don't label. Just be open. If you don't connect with someone, then move on. It's fine. I would like you to practice your networking. So go out and talk to one person at the school playground who you haven't spoken to before. Smile at them, say 'Hi', then introduce yourself and see where it goes.

When I arrived in Australia, I had no local connections so I had to work at making them. From the experience of previous moves, the best way of doing this was by offering help.

Shortly after my son started school, the school newsletter mentioned that the Parent & Friend Association were looking for new members. I figured it was a good way of learning how Australian schools operated and to be involved in my son's school so I went along with a curious mind and came away as a co-convenor!

Did I do the greatest job? Not really because I was still finding my feet in terms of cultural and local knowledge but I gave it a go. Out of that one foray into networking came friendships which are still there eight years on along with its benefits like job opportunities, social invitations, local knowledge and a sense of purpose.

What to Do: Step 2

Another great way to expand your network is to join external social or activity groups. It may be something that piques your interest or something that you have done previously and enjoyed. It could be an evening class, a committee for a cause which you support, a walking group or even an online course or forum. Often, networking on the internet can lead to social networking like meeting up once a month at a restaurant.

I joined a book club not long after I arrived in Australia and it has been fantastic. We're very different women who come from different walks of life so I get all sorts of viewpoints from different people and read books that I may never have considered.

We go away for a weekend once a year and always plan a gourmet lunch for one of the days. As a group, we also see films, especially ones based on the books we've read. A whole new social life came out of just one group that meets so many of my interests: reading, debating, food and film. It has also been a privilege to connect to a group of wonderfully supportive women.

What to Do: Step 3

Finally, find someone who you can truly connect with at school. You are going to be attached to the school for a number of years so connecting with another parent will give you common ground and your paths will cross with a regularity that makes the relationship easy to maintain.

This may not happen instantly. You might have a couple of false starts but I can guarantee you that there will be someone in that playground who you can connect with. You become each other's sounding board, confidante and an all-round great team. You will have each other's back on those bad days and will also lose count of the laughs, tears and glasses of wine that you share. There's a chance that it will be a lifelong connection.

When my son first started school in England, I kept seeing this lady who always sported a short, brightly coloured hairstyle and who was always laughing and happy. There was just something about her which made me curious.

It took me a while to pluck up the courage to speak to her as she seemed so popular and my 'little me' voices insisted that she wouldn't be interested in me. That was fourteen years ago and we are still going strong despite the distance of over 10,000 miles! This amazing woman has generously given me her friendship, encouragement, time, knowledge, passion, not to mention generous measures of wine and laughter!

Networking may be something you're feeling uncomfortable with now. It might be something you wouldn't ordinarily consider doing. You might just want to run and hide from the world. It's not the end of the world if it doesn't work, so just move on. But you don't know what may come from it if you don't try.

Nice Try but I've Heard It Before

One excuse I hear constantly is, 'I don't have the time for networking.' My response is, 'How are you spending your time?' If your children are at school, if you've got a sense of isolation, then that suggests you've got time on your hands to have those negative thoughts.

It doesn't matter if it's half an hour or half a day, there will be time for you to connect with other people. School pickup is an ideal time to start and it only takes five minutes. Start slowly and gradually build those connections and relationships.

Another key argument is, 'I'm not really a social person, I'm quite an introvert.' Really? You never socialise with your family? You never had a friend or attended a social event? Everyone has some sort of social element in their life, be it a family gathering or attending a school production. No one stands completely in isolation and if joining a group feels a little unfamiliar, that's fine. You can just chat to one person and build it up slowly as your confidence grows. You don't have to walk straight into a group.

I used to have quite a mindset around mothers: *Oh, I don't do mums. They can be boring and just want to talk about their kids.* Well, labelling is a trap you can fall into so don't make assumptions. Just think, you're a mum but you're not boring. You're an intelligent, creative human being and so are all the other mums out there. Don't stereotype. There will be people who you don't connect with, who happen to also be mums and that's fine. Don't forget it works the other way around too!

Your Key Actions and Learnings

1. Utilise what you already have access to and practice.

2. Do something new and different like joining a new group.

3. Establish and develop a key connection.

Research is formalised curiosity. It is poking and prying with a purpose.

Zora Neale Hurston

10. On a Mission to Succeed

– The Need for Research

Ideas, concepts and projects rarely just happen on their own. They need research behind them so you can work out the 'how' of making something happen. Research is investigating and gathering information from various reliable and reputable sources in order to gain knowledge as well as generating strategies that will propel you forward.

When doing research, you are creating the framework and giving yourself the needed clarity to make a start on a project or idea. You see your idea evolve and take shape. Also, the more research you do, the more it generates new ideas. You may see possibilities that you hadn't seen before.

As you carry on with your research, the facts and information you gather give you certainty. You go from *Can I do it?* and *I'm not sure* to *Now I know I can*. The more facts and evidence you have to support your ideas, the less excuse you have for not acting.

What I absolutely love about doing research is that not only does it give you a sense of purpose and momentum but it also leads you to taking action. One thing leads to another. For example, you might be interested in starting up a charity event so you go online and search for ideas. Next, you email and call friends to see if they will get involved. Soon, things snowball and you are running and hosting the event. Getting into research mode gets your idea out of your head and into existence.

Doing research can save you time and money in the long run. It gives you the opportunity to see what's available, the general costs, the time required and so on. If you are starting a microbusiness, then you check out some of the pitfalls, legalities and requirements that you need to be aware of. Time and again, I have seen people flounder and stall because they haven't invested time in researching their project.

If you don't do the research, you're setting yourself up to fail. By not taking the steps to move forward, you are unlikely to ever get your idea out of your head. It's going to remain a dream. You may waste your valuable time or make costly mistakes by spending time and money on things that you don't want, don't work and don't deliver the results.

Worse still, you may end up making legal mistakes if you are starting a small business and that could cost you not just money but also your business and credibility. Spend time on research; it can save you time, it can save you money and it can save you from heartache.

What to Do: Step 1

One of the key things around research is to utilise technology. Make it your best friend. We have so much information at our fingertips. There are plenty of social-media groups, forums, search engines and online directories. It's never been easier to research things. The advantage of doing online research is that it can reduce the legwork and save valuable time.

Use the internet as your starting point. If you need supplies, then run a search on suppliers and see what's out there and where they are. Ask other people who are in a similar area. What do they do? Where do they go? Who do they use? All this can be done online.

When I moved to Australia, I struggled with finding decent jewellery suppliers and it wasn't cost- and time-effective to remain with my trusted UK suppliers. So I utilised the internet as my first point of call, looked at the sites to determine their stock and honed it down.

I got an idea of who stocked what and I knew what I needed so I ruled out the ones that just weren't going to work for me. Then I visited the ones I was left with as I prefer to actually see and touch what I am buying, as well as being able to build relationships with my stockists.

So, write down all the ideas you have about creating a project for yourself or a microbusiness. If it's a long list, then pick your top three. Create your actions list and start researching.

Keep chipping away a little bit each day. You don't have to do all the research in one hit but you may find that it gets addictive! You can do a little bit so it doesn't feel like an insurmountable task. Half an hour per day and swap your reality-TV fix for creating your reality is all you need to get started.

What to Do: Step 2

Having waxed lyrical about the benefits of using the internet to do your research, be mindful that there are cowboys out there.

I always say, 'Don't take everything at face value.' The internet is just a tool so always ask questions. If you're seeking services, then ask what that person has done to make them the expert. What can they offer you? What are the benefits? Do they have testimonials? Do they have clients who you can speak to?

I tend to not believe anything until I've got tangible evidence. It probably is a bit cynical of me but that's my strategy and it works well for me, especially when it comes to investing a lot of money.

When I was looking at enhancing my coaching qualifications, because it's an unregulated industry, I was particularly cautious as I had learnt the hard way that there can be smoke and mirrors in the web world.

A few years ago in the UK, the first college I signed up for looked impressive online and the consultants on the phone talked the talk and convinced me that they were the right college. However, partway through the course, the company went bankrupt.

Luckily, I had already attended the training course so it wasn't a complete loss of money. But there were people who were affected financially. I learnt a valuable lesson about what questions I should have been asking rather than being swayed by what I wanted to hear.

When I wanted to add to my qualifications, I did a lot of research and did it differently. I had telephone conversations and I visited the college and met with some of the staff. I discovered, quite accidentally, on the website that one of their past students was a mum at my daughter's school. I got in contact with her and asked her what her experiences were. Through this, I gained much better evidence and knowledge to base my decision on.

So, do ask questions and don't just blindly accept what's out there especially for big investments of time and money.

Get into the practice of developing a list of questions that you need to ask so that you have a starting point when you call or visit people. For me, if I don't write them down, then nine times out of ten, I'll come off the phone or out of the meeting having forgotten to ask something.

What to Do: Step 3

You may need to do what I call 'internal research'. For example, you might have a general idea of what you want to do. You visualise wanting to spend four hours a day creating beautiful products to sell. You've managed to get it down to one or two interests or you've got a couple of hobbies that feed into that visualisation but you cannot quite pin it down.

I suggest you experiment and try different things until you find something that you love doing and are confident that you can do well enough to produce to sell.

Whilst I did have a clear idea about making jewellery, I constantly did my own internal research. I've tried different classes and different methodologies to find out if there are other aspects of jewellery-making that I might enjoy doing.

Be open to things that you may not have previously considered. For me, I have always thought of quilting as being too *Chintzy* but then I thought, *Why does it have to be chintzy? I love bold colours and textures so why can't I use that in quilting?*

I discovered a brilliant teacher who ran a fabulous course and was encouraging of the things that I wanted to do. As a result of being receptive to trying something I had preconceived ideas about, I discovered that I absolutely loved quilting. Open up to possibilities and you may be surprised what comes out of it.

Remember, it's a journey and it's your journey. If you don't have the immediate ideas around what you want to do, then that's absolutely fine. There's no time limit on this. You don't have to get to your destination within a week. It's as long as you need it to be, provided you are taking action.

Nice Try but I've Heard It Before

My clients often say, 'You know, I've got so many ideas, I just don't know where to start.'

That's fantastic! Go you! Start by jotting them all down. Writing them out and seeing them on paper helps give you clarity. When you get it out of your head, you get a feel for which ideas you are enthused about. Pick your top idea and break it down into your initial steps of what you need to research. Find out more and determine when you're going to do it by.

Some people get a little fazed about the internet. They get overwhelmed by the amount of information that they just give up looking. There is an abundance of information out there but don't let that put you off. You can make your searches very specific, so don't just put 'painting classes'. Put in something more specific like 'daytime beginner's oil painting class in Melbourne'.

The more you practice searching, the quicker you get to sort out the search results. You develop your own style of searching. I can quickly glance over the search results and pick out the key words that I know I'm looking for and dismiss the ones that I think aren't relevant.

Of course, time is always thrown into the pot. 'I haven't got time to visit people or locations.' I get that. Most of us haven't got oodles of spare time so that's why I advise you to be clear on what you need. Do what you can from home such as asking questions on the phone and then narrow your choices down. That way, when you do go make a visit, you've done the groundwork.

Remember, not everything requires a visit. Some things can be dealt with over the phone or ordered online quite confidently. You don't actually need that much time to go out. Just visit the key, important areas.

Your Key Actions and Learnings

1. Get your top ideas sussed out. Develop an action plan and start researching.

2. Develop a list of questions.

3. Do an internal research audit.

'Poirot,' I said. 'I have been thinking.'
'An admirable exercise my friend. Continue it.'
Agatha Christie, *Peril at End House*

11. Thinking Outside the Box
– Creating a Microbusiness

For many mums, despite having to give up full-time work in the corporate world, they start to consider the possibility of going back to work after a few years but not to their previous roles.

They want something which enables them to contribute financially and as a means to gain independence but, more fundamentally and importantly, they want stimulation outside of their family home. They don't want to go back to the corporate world because that doesn't fit in with their current family life. Then they discover that part-time jobs are pretty thin on the ground and, quite often, are beneath their capabilities.

I was shocked when I looked around for work. If I wanted a part-time role, then it definitely meant stepping down the ladder. If I wanted a role that matched my abilities or financial expectations, then I was going to have to commute and sacrifice family time by doing long days. I also discovered the sort of discrimination that women can face when returning to work post-children. The whole process was a demoralising eye-opener.

Given all that was far from ideal, I explored the possibility of starting my own microbusiness. I wasn't looking to become the next Anita Roddick or Arianna Huffington.

I just wanted to establish something that fed into my creativity but also helped me earn some income. I wanted to have the flexibility to be there for my children when I wanted to be there and when they needed me.

Starting a microbusiness is pretty easy. It's about having the willingness to try new things. You may need to compromise when necessary and embrace uncertainty, yet, paradoxically, you'll have the absolute certainty that you'll increase your experience and confidence as a result of having a go. If that sounds like something you're prepared to do, then a microbusiness may be the option for you.

Having a microbusiness gives you flexibility as you decide your hours and where you work. Furthermore, the possibilities are limited only by you. You can be artistic or you can utilise specific skills, such as accounting, bookkeeping and typing. Or it can be community-based such as teaching gym classes, being a child minder or a party planner.

Going solo is going to give you different experiences. You're going to find yourself dealing with different people and perhaps exploring different fields of work that you haven't considered before. It will give you a sense of achievement, give you more confidence and improve your attitude.

You'll be stretching yourself and acquiring new skills. You will learn new things in areas which you know so you're expanding your knowledge. Perhaps you were a bookkeeper and now you've acquired the skills to become an accountant. You may have loved yoga and then qualify to become a yoga teacher.

You might do party planning and then you're speaking to groups and your public speaking skills improve. Everything brings experience regardless of whether it's your 'chosen' path or not.

As you generate your own income stream, not only does your confidence in your abilities grow but so does your sense of achievement and independence.

More importantly, you can have low start-up costs depending on what you choose to do. You don't have to invest lots of money immediately. There are lots of resources out there that are free or are very low cost, giving you the option to dip your toes in and have a go.

You might already be an expert in a particular area so it's then about getting the word out there. It can be a small ad in a local paper or just some networking to let people know that you're doing business or using a cheap print company to get business cards and leaflets out there. You can also utilise the services of freelance experts through sites such as Elance or Fiverr or if you feel confident in your own design skills, there are plenty of websites or computer programs where you can create your own marketing materials.

A recent 2015 report for the Department of Business Innovation and Skills found that mothers returning to work at any level face discrimination.[2] They can be dismissed, made redundant or treated so poorly that they quit their jobs. To me, it's a no-brainer. Why put yourself through that unnecessary stress when there are so many options to starting a microbusiness and retaining your own independence and control?

---

[2] The Department for Business, Innovation and Skills (BIS) and the Equality and Human Rights Commission (EHRC), *Pregnancy and Maternity-Related Discrimination and Disadvantage, First findings: Surveys of Employers and Mothers*, BIS Research Paper No. 235, IFF Research, BIS and EHRC, UK, viewed September 2016,

https://www.gov.uk/government/uploads/system/uploads/attachment_data/file/465930/BIS-15-447-pregnancy-and-maternity-related-discrimination-and-disadvantage.pdf.

What's the difference between a microbusiness and a small business? A microbusiness is normally run by one person who may have one to two employees but essentially is a one-man band. A small business can include up to forty staff members.

What to Do: Step 1

So how do you go about starting or even thinking about a microbusiness?

I suggest you first 'design' your business day. I find it useful to use a combination of visualisation, writing lists and brainstorming ideas on paper. How many hours do you want to work? When do you want to work? Do you want to work at home or do you need a studio? Are you sharing a project with someone? Are you choosing to utilise a hobby and turn that into a business where you're making things to sell? Or would it be a little less creative and more practical like a cleaning business or a child-minding business? Are you prepared to retrain or advance current skills?

Be very clear on what it is you want out of your business. What compromises are you prepared to make? How much family time do you want? How much business time do you want? What kind of income/profit do you want to achieve?

Get that framework in place so you know what options are open, what's negotiable and what's not. It's like a birth plan. It's great to have but don't be too rigid. Unexpected things can and do happen so a bit of flexibility can go a long way.

When I started selling my jewellery, a friend suggested we do jewellery parties for children. Thankfully, we did a trial run with our friend's kids and set about making bracelets with beads and elastic. But I had never worked with that elastic medium and neither of us could work out how to knot it so that it didn't come undone.

It wasn't a disaster. The kids had fun, we had a bit of a giggle and I learnt a lot from that session including the fact that I prefer working solo when it comes to making jewellery. Since I was not rigid in my expected outcomes, I could see the event for what it was: a valuable learning experience but not an avenue which I wanted to continue down. For the record, I can now knot elastic successfully!

And don't forget, nothing has to be forever. Just be open to ideas as there can be different stepping stones to get to your ideal microbusiness dependent on your circumstances. When a friend first suggested that I try child-minding, I threw my hands up in horror at the thought of looking after other people's children. Yet, a couple of months down the track, there I was doing exactly that.

I knew that it was not my dream business but at that point in time it gave me much of what I wanted from a micro business: flexibility, an income, home based, autonomy, and was quick to start up. I gained valuable training, skills, business acumen, as well as new social connections. So whilst I knew this was not the end game, it sure as hell beat the corporate alternatives.

What to Do: Step 2

Once you have your framework, find out about the non-negotiables, the things that you have to have in place or have knowledge about such as tax implications, insurance and public liability. Does your car insurance have to change? Does your house insurance have to change?

Different businesses require different things. Find out

about the legalities. Do you need certain registrations or certifications? What are the council requirements? If you're setting up a dog-boarding business, you probably have to check with the council regarding the number of dogs you're allowed to look after.

There is lots of free business help and advice out there. There are online advice organisations for small businesses. Have a look at www.enterprisenation.com or flyingsolo.com.au. Government websites are also a great source of guidance. Local councils often run cheap or subsidised courses on running your business and some councils even offer subsidised mentoring sessions. Check out your local library and see what advice/guide books they have available. I have always found the *For Dummies* guide books really useful.

As you can see, there is advice out there that doesn't have to cost you a fortune. I strongly advise you to invest time in this to prevent costly mistakes down the track.

What to Do: Step 3

Finally, look at what I call the peripherals. The business cards, website, stationary, equipment, social media and so forth. Be very clear on what it is you need versus what you want. It's very easy to get carried away and excited with all the nice, shiny stuff and buy lots of new things.

Think very carefully and don't invest too much money initially in the nice-to-haves but just invest in the need-to-haves. You don't need to have everything at once. There are lots of free or low-cost things that you can utilise such as social media.

What tools are essential to have? What specific stock do you need to get you started? Do you need a laptop? Is it going to be a PC or a Mac? Do you need a sewing machine? Do you need a desk? Can you start at the kitchen table? Do you have a space that you can identify as a business area if you're working from home? If you do need studio space or office space, can you share the cost with someone else and work out a roster for using it?

Be practical, be resourceful and just be very clear about the reason for getting something. You don't want to be spending too much money until you start bringing in an income.

I wanted a good quality website that would not just speak about me but also my services. Realistically, I didn't have the budget for what I wanted but I already had the logo files and I was happy to write the content. So I negotiated a good deal and got the website which I wanted and felt would serve my business well.

When it comes to my desire for antique architect drawers for storing all my beads and silver in, I can't justify the purchase. They are expensive, I don't have the space and what I currently have is serviceable. It's a nice-to-have but not a need-to-have. For the time being, it will remain on my wish list.

Nice Try but I've Heard It Before

One of the questions I often get is, 'How am I going to find the time to start up a business?' I would reply, 'If you were thinking of working, where would you find the time to go back to work?'

A microbusiness based at home is going to be arguably easier to find time for because you're not commuting anywhere. Starting a business is part of the 'doing' of a business. Remember, this is about being flexible and knowing that you may have to compromise for a while.

If that means you're typing up a proposal at ten o'clock at night so that you can be available to assist in the classroom during the day, then so be it. It's setting the foundation for your future business and freedom.

People often worry that their business may be a failure. Well, nothing's ever a failure. You're always going to learn from what you've done. You'll either learn to adjust what you're doing by seeking professional help or you can move onto the next thing. Look at what you've done, what you've learnt and how can you do it differently. Nothing is ever a failure. It's all experience that can move you forward.

I also get asked, 'How much money do I need for a start-up?' The question you should be asking is, 'How little can I do this for?' You can always justify a purchase in some manner if you really want to but whether it's required is something else.

Just as you probably manage the house finances by creating a budget, do the same thing with your business. Set up a budget and shop around for your prices. Decide where money can't be scrimped on, such as public liability insurance and save on areas such as business cards.

Companies such as Vistaprint do budget deals and the quality is acceptable. Be clear on your budget and stick to it. As I mentioned earlier, it can be as expensive as you want or as cost-effective as you need it to be.

Your Key Actions and Learnings

1. Write down how you want your business day to look.

2. Invest time in finding out what you have to have, such as insurance etc.

3. Draw up two lists, one for the actual needs of the business and one for the nice-to-haves. The latter you can use as motivation since you can buy an item when you have achieved some of your goals.

A true teacher would never tell you what to do. But he would give you the knowledge with which you could decide what would be best for you to do.

Christopher Pike, *Sati*

12. Calling in the Experts
– Getting a Coach Onboard

No one knows you better than you.

And that is the basic premise that life coaches work on. You are your own expert.

Nevertheless, we all need a helping hand now and again to bring out the best in us. Just as you go to a GP to get a diagnosis on an ailment or a teacher to gain the knowledge you need, a coach can help you find the resources that you already have to create the best version of you.

Of course, it's not compulsory but where else do you get a judgement-free space to be listened to and actually be heard?

Coaching is a conversation unlike any that you would have had. It's not an ordinary conversation but one that will challenge your thinking. A coach will ask questions that are going to create change. They will stretch and challenge you. The conversation will disrupt your thinking and create new perspectives. It's not about pandering your ego but rather ruffling your feathers and getting you to think outside the box and rearranging those feathers.

Coaching also offers a different approach to some other methodologies and therapies. It concentrates on the future as opposed to the past and, because of this, it may be faster than some other therapies.

As coaches will offer different ways to look at situations, you will have new perspectives on the way you think. As a consequence, you start having insight and clarity around your own patterns of thinking and behaviour.

As the wheels and cogs in your head turn, you make connections on how your responses and behaviour have influenced your outcomes and the reactions you may have received from others. With these new realisations, you can make the necessary changes to improve certain areas of your life.

Life coaches will also hold you accountable for any goals and plans you make. It's not enough to discover and talk about what you want moving forward. You will need to take some action outside of your sessions and, as coaches, we are not going to let you off the hook that easily!

We commit 100% to your success and part of that can mean calling you out on what you haven't done as much as what you have. Provided that you are committed to the coaching process, you will find that you start to take the steps needed to create the change you want.

The best 'Aha' moments and insights often happen outside the coaching session when you reflect on what has been said, so don't always expect it to end after your session. As a result, you will develop your own sense of accountability and your own process of reflection which makes you responsible for

12. Calling in the Experts

all that you do and prevents you from going down the path of external blaming.

Research commissioned by the International Coaching Federation shows that 99% of people who were coached were either somewhat or very satisfied with the overall experience.[3]

So, you're kind of in a win-win situation. You're going to get results and you're going to be happy with the process. Just like leaving a health problem unchecked, by not investing in some coaching sessions, your current situation may not improve or may even get worse. You may remain stuck with no clear direction or strategies to help create change in your life.

At the very best, you may find your solutions but it will take you a lot longer to get there. Let's face it, life is short. Wouldn't you want to take the quickest route to the better version of you?

So what exactly is life coaching? It's a relationship in which the coach looks at what is happening right now for the client and utilises communication skills such as questioning, listening and clarifying to facilitate new strategies and shift-thinking in order to move forward in a chosen area or goal.

What to Do: Step 1

You've made your decision and you would like to have a coaching session or two. That's fantastic and well done for taking charge of your life.

I would like to point out that coaching is not currently a regulated industry, so do your research. Ask questions, such

---

[3] ICF, 'Need Coaching? The benefits coaching can have on your organization', viewed September 2016, https://www.coachfederation.org/files/FileDownloads/NeedCoaching.pdf

as what qualifications the coach has and what qualifications they have over and above coaching.

It's good to have someone who's got a holistic approach so what other areas have they studied? What other qualifications do they have which may be relevant to your needs? Not only are you getting a broader knowledge base but it also demonstrates that they are committed to their own ongoing professional development.

What life experiences do they have? If you're looking for someone to help you create a microbusiness post-corporate life, then you may want someone who has gone through that journey and achieved the success which you are seeking. That way, they are going to have a deeper understanding of what is needed to achieve your goals. I would also ask if they have testimonials and recommendations.

Ask if they abide by some sort of Code of Ethics and Standards. Request a copy. There are a couple of institutions, like the International Coaching Federation and International Coach Guild, which have good comprehensive ethics and standards. It's good to know what the benchmarks are and what you should be looking for.

As I've mentioned before, things can look good on a website or on a piece of paper, so go in deep and ask questions. Any coach worth their salt will be more than happy to answer your questions.

But remember, all the qualifications, testimonials and references in the world do not matter if they are not a fit for you. Many coaches offer a free initial session or an in-depth chat. Take advantage of this. Have a list of questions ready for the coach. Do they do coaching face to face, on Skype or via telephone? What's going to work best for you?

Some people prefer to be coached over the phone to save them travelling whilst others prefer face-to-face coaching. You might not know how you like to be coached, so what do they offer? Do they offer lots of different methods of coaching? Do you get email support? What are their hours of operation? Do they fit in with your lifestyle and schedule?

What to Do: Step 2

Have a good idea of what outcomes you would like to achieve through coaching. Whilst the journey may take you to unexpected places, it is good to be clear on what you want from your sessions. Coaches are not mind-readers. Well, sometimes we are but not always so please let us know what you are hoping to gain and achieve.

As you go through the session, take ownership of how you want to be coached as well. It might be that you need someone to be quite firm with you or you may prefer a gentle approach. It's fine to ask for that.

When I was first being coached, I didn't feel like the coach was really listening to me and didn't really get me. As a coach myself, I knew I had to take responsibility for how I wanted to be coached. So, I relayed what I needed and they took this onboard and some great results came out of it. Take that as an 'insider' tip because clients are often not aware that they can make requests.

Let me put it another way. It's like going to a hairdresser you're unfamiliar with. You go in, you get a cut but you're not really happy with the result. You feel a bit embarrassed and awkward to say anything so you leave the salon disappointed and know that you won't go back.

However, if you had actually said to the hairdresser, 'Hey, I'm not quite sure about this. Could you do it slightly different?'

then they would have been happy to adjust their work. They would want you to leave the salon happy with what they have done and you've taken ownership for what has happened. It's the same thing with coaching.

What to Do: Step 3

You've had some sessions and you may even think your coach is the greatest thing since sliced bread but, besides the actual coaching, what's on offer that will add value to your growth? Do you get recordings of your sessions? Most coaches are happy to provide that for you.

Do they offer workshops, books and online courses? It's always great to dip in and out of different styles of teaching to enhance your learning. I love having manuals or books to refer to and workshops have been wonderful spaces to learn and connect with like-minded people.

I attended a morning cushion-making course a while back and liked this person's method of teaching and personality. So when they offered a one-day retreat to do something else at a different location, I immediately jumped onboard. It was great to be with a familiar teacher in a different space. I learnt some new techniques and also received a handout for referencing so that I could continue with the project and embark on a new one.

So see what else is on offer. It's only going to enhance your learning.

Nice Try but I've Heard It Before

One of the things that people put up as resistance to getting a coach is that they don't have money for coaching. Like most things in life, we make a decision on what our priorities are and what we are prepared to invest in.

12. Calling in the Experts

What we spend our money on is a good indicator of what our priorities are. After the essentials such as mortgage, food and clothing, where is your money going? How much do you want to invest in yourself?

People often say, 'Well, how do I know coaching works?' You will know by your results. And your results will be determined by your commitment to the coaching process. A coach cannot make you have results. They can facilitate your change and engage you in new perspectives and strategies but, ultimately, you are responsible for your results.

A lot of people feel uncomfortable disclosing personal stuff and that's natural. You're on the precipice of confronting your hidden self so make sure you pick a coach who you feel comfortable with.

If you feel really uncomfortable with disclosing personal stuff, that's fine. Consider attending a group workshop which can be a good springboard into deeper stuff. It's a bit more comfortable and not so confronting. It will still get your thought processes going and there will be lots of helpful tips and strategies about how to change your thinking, so try that as an alternative to one-on-one coaching.

Your Key Actions and Learnings

1. Do your research and ask questions.

2. Be clear on your outcomes and what you want from coaching.

3. Ask what else is on offer.

Afterword

Brilliant! You've made it through to the other side. Congratulations! How amazing do you look and feel? What incredible things are you telling yourself after this crazy journey?

I trust that you now have more clarity and direction having read through the reasons why you felt like you did and how you can take the steps needed to create a more positive lifestyle.

In the preceding chapters, you have learnt how to get that positive mindset, make fear your best friend, get the key ingredients of your personality, utilise them resourcefully and install positive beliefs to support you as well as how to go about 'doing the do'!

If you find yourself slipping back into your old ways, think about how far you have come with some simple adjustments to your thinking and actions. What will it cost you to go back to being the person who was stuck, not knowing who you were and where you were going? You now have the knowledge and the certainty that you can do this.

So, trust that you have got this and, failing that, pick this book up and remind yourself. And remember: consistency, not complacency, is the key to your ongoing development and growth.

I feel like I have been on a journey with you throughout these pages and that is such a privileged space to be in, so thank you and here's to your continued success.

Whilst this is the end of the book, I know that this is not the end of your journey. I would absolutely love to hear from you and know what has changed as a result of you reading this book.

Feel free to drop me a line at: michelle@growwithmk.com

Testimonials (continued)

Michelle's approach in all the sessions was calm and considered. I felt safe to open up to her and talk honestly. She listened carefully and was compassionate but also did not allow me to ramble. She was firm and caring.

At times, the questions she posed were very difficult and confronting but these always contributed most to me. These sessions were amazingly productive and I managed to get things done that I had been meaning to do for a long time. I am still not entirely sure how it happened.

Michelle taught me how to accurately visualise myself when a goal had been reached. This technique took away the whole concept of 'goals' for me. Goals have always been something on a 'to-do' list. If I visualise how it will be, then I can place myself there, like it's real. It's so much more inspiring than looking at a list and that's important in a creative occupation.

Michelle also helped me to identify reoccurring patterns in my behaviour that stop me from getting things done, particularly procrastination and allowing fears to rule me. As someone who works alone and who had the sense of the world going on without me, I am amazed that something led me to get up in front of a crowd at a seminar. I faced that fear, but also afterwards I had to choose whether or not to listen to that voice that tried to tell me I had made an idiot of myself.

It is not easy to acknowledge yourself wholeheartedly for your achievements but Michelle has taught me that it's important. It gives you a springboard to keep going. It has also contributed to our family life as I have recognized how good it feels to be acknowledged, so I make a conscious effort to let people know I appreciate them.

Lastly, Michelle taught me that thinking positively isn't just an idea to try out now and again. It's a muscle that needs to be exercised and it works well if you choose to use it. Being conscious of that choice is something I hope will stay with me.

Michelle has contributed more to me than she will ever know. Her commitment to people is beautiful. It seems silly to say, 'I wish her well in her career choice' as I am already certain that she will be absolutely brilliant at it.

– Karen Erasmus
Illustrator

Michelle has been able to assist me on several occasions when I had met stumbling blocks on my new pathway to developing myself in my new career.

I was met with several personal and work-related challenges and often felt overwhelmed and confused about how to address my aims and goals. Michelle was able to pinpoint and ask thought-provoking questions that allowed me to think deeper. What did I want to achieve? What were my true values and sentiments? How would I order those values within my company and my life?

I was then able to objectively look at different aspects of who I was and how I could best move forward. The path became clearer and I am still often able to return to our original coaching conversations and gain clarity in my decisions and actions.

Michelle has a unique way of prompting and quizzing

that is friendly but direct which opens doorways into your own thoughts. This allows you to consider objectively the reasons behind why you may feel or act in a certain way. Michelle was able to successfully lead and guide every time we met and I value her help. It has allowed me to look with a clearer perspective at my business and at my values as well as assisting with preparing and planning my goals.

– Jo Bates
Crazy Canines, Dog Behaviour & Training Consultant

Michelle conducted a group training session for my boot-camp participants on the Why Factor. This helped them to get a much better understanding of their personal selves on why they workout and all the benefits it offers.

I found the experience professional, very beneficial and interesting as Michelle shared a personal experience which we could relate to and, at the same time, felt a closer connection with her.

– Michelle
Total Reshape

I immediately found Michelle very easy to communicate with on a personal level.

Michelle helped me to find a new direction and set goals that would best suit my life situation.

I value the insight Michelle helped me gain in achieving my future endeavours and highly recommend her as a coach.

– Trent Lawson

I was feeling unfulfilled and I wanted to find something to add purpose to my life.

Both my boys were happily settled at school so it was now time for me to consider my future. I had, years earlier, completed three years of a four-year psychology course but that was so long ago.

Being very interested in food values and healthy eating, I decided to study nutrition. I lacked the confidence to take the first step and this was when Michelle was my saviour. She inspired me, made me believe in myself and supported my decision to enrol in a Certificate of Nutrition.

Without Michelle's input, I would still be floundering and I intend to move happily and confidently ahead with my chosen course.

I sincerely thank Michelle and highly recommend her coaching methods.
  – Georgie Merks

I was a year-12 student finding the assignments and SACs all very overwhelming. Time was running out, my exams were about to commence and I knew I needed some guidance. So I asked Michelle for help. She was willing to take an hour out of her day once per week to work with me.

Michelle provided me with useful ideas and techniques such as mind maps, bubbles of quotes and appropriate grammar. We would always break things down into easier steps which would help with my memory. All of a sudden, my grades were going from C's to B's, something I never thought I'd see. Those few months in my last year of schooling became easier and less stressful thanks to Michelle.

Michelle always checked in to see how I was coping. She'd give me homework and small tasks to help me stay on top of the workload. I now know that organisation is the key and to never say, 'I'll try,' but rather to say, 'I'm going to.'

I highly recommend any student going through tough times in their studies to be coached by Michelle as she is fantastic. I wouldn't hesitate to work with Michelle again to overcome any difficult challenges I may face in the future.
  – Laura Deeley

About the Author

Michelle Kuklinski was born in London, is a mother to an amazing son and daughter and a serial experimenter. She loves to try new and different things from craft to cooking, cultural experiences to challenging reading and trying new hair colours! Along with her family, she moved to Australia in 2008 and now resides in Melbourne.

Prior to family life, Michelle was active in the corporate world, mainly in the banking and oil industry. Family life brought about a change of priorities and, whilst she was determined to be around for her family, Michelle always knew that she wouldn't be content with that as her sole role.

For a short time, Michelle returned to the corporate world but the demands and some of the values did not suit her life at that point. Hence, she became a serial entrepreneur creating business opportunities that fitted in with her other life commitments.

So, whilst finishing a degree in psychosocial studies and also becoming a credentialed coaching practitioner, she grew her list of expertise and successes in other areas: party plan consultant, day-care provider, jewellery designer and writer. If Michelle thought she could do it, enjoy it and bring something to others, then she did it!

Michelle has always been curious about human behaviour and what makes us tick; after all, everyone's favourite subject is 'me'. She constantly heard many mums lament that they love their children but missed what working life gave them. At the same time, they did not want to go back to that 'old world'. She thought, *I know what you mean, I've been there, felt the pain and got the t-shirt.* But she also realised that she had found different ways of navigating the maze of motherhood whilst sustaining her own desire to have something outside of being a mum.

That was Michelle's 'light bulb' moment: if she could do it, then so can others and, if they are not able to, then she can help them. Hence GrowwithMK was born in 2014, a coaching company that utilises creativity, human behaviour expertise and experience in facilitating resourceful solutions to that confusing dilemma which often comes up for women raising families: 'What about me?'

www.growwithmk.com

michelle@growwithmk.com

Exclusive Offer

For the Readers of Beyond the School Gate

Moving Beyond Mum Exploration Session

Are you ready to commit to 'you' and take it to the next level?

You know with absolute certainty that you want to see serious results and live your ideal life that doesn't reduce you to being 'just a mum'.

Reading this book has given you the framework to start this process but will not hold you accountable for your actions nor help you maintain your momentum. This exclusive package will give you two 1-hour sessions with Michelle during which you will come away with:

- Your unique personality recipe
- A clear vision for your future
- A precise action plan for your first steps in creating change
- Emails to keep you motivated and accountable
- A copy of *Feel the Fear and Do it Anyway* by Susan Jeffers.

The total value is $597 but your investment is just $97.

Please email info@growwithmk.com with the subject line 'Book Unpack Special' and mention in the main body of the email that you saw this package in this book.